Practice *Makes* **Perfect**

Idiomatic English

≈≈≈

A Workbook for Mastering
Adjective Phrases • Noun Phrases
Prepositional Phrases • Verb Phrases

Loretta S. Gray

Mc
Graw
Hill

New York Chicago San Francisco Lisbon London Madrid Mexico City
Milan New Delhi San Juan Seoul Singapore Sydney Toronto

The McGraw·Hill Companies

I am very grateful to everyone who helped put this text together:
in particular, Richard Spears, who inspired the idea for the project;
Mary Jane Maples, who encouraged me to pursue the project; and
Paula Eacott and Robert Schnelle, who offered valuable comments on early drafts.

I would also like to thank Patsy Callaghan and the Office of Graduate Studies and
Research at Central Washington University for allowing me time to write.

9 10 11 12 13 14 15 16 17 18 19 20 21 22 23 24 25 26   QDB/QDB   1 9 8 7 6 5 4 3 2 1

ISBN 978-0-8442-2394-0
MHID   0-8442-2394-8

Library of Congress Cataloging-in-Publication Data

Gray, Loretta S.
    Practice makes perfect : idiomatic English : a workbook for mastering adjective phrases, noun phrases, prepositional phrases, verb phrases / Loretta S. Gray.
        p.   cm.
    Includes index.
    ISBN 0-8442-2394-8
    1. English language—Textbooks for foreign speakers.   2. English language—Idioms—Problems, exercises, etc.   3. English language—Grammar—Problems, exercises, etc.   4. English language—Terms and phrases—Problems, exercises, etc.   I. Title: Idiomatic English.   II. Title.

PE1128.G6565   2000
428.3'4—dc21   99-49998
                                                        CIP

Cover design by Amy Yu Ng

McGraw-Hill books are available at special quantity discounts to use as premiums and sales promotions or for use in corporate training programs. To contact a representative, please e-mail us at bulksales@mcgraw-hill.com.

This book is printed on acid-free paper.

Contents

Introduction   v

A   Adjective Phrases   1

   1   Enchantment   3
   2   Satisfaction   9
   3   Work   15
   4   Connections   20
   5   Turmoil   25
   6   Attraction   30
   7   School   35
   8   Talent   40
   9   Kindness   45
  10   Travel   50
  11   Trouble   55

B   Noun Phrases   61

   1   Family Life   63
   2   Entertainment   68
   3   Language Learning   73
   4   Employment   78
   5   Harm and Safety   83
   6   Friends and Enemies   88
   7   Education   94
   8   Business   100
   9   Health   106
  10   Science and Technology   111
  11   Economy   117

C   Prepositional Phrases   123

   1   Time   125
   2   Sequence   130
   3   Buying and Selling   135
   4   Similarities and Differences   140
   5   Health   145

	6	Entertainment	150
	7	Perspectives	155
	8	Process	160
	9	Location	165
	10	Exceptions and Substitutions	170
	11	Decisions	175
	12	Reference	180

D   Verb Phrases   185

	1	Friends	187
	2	School	192
	3	Working Together	197
	4	Shopping	202
	5	Dating	207
	6	Travel	213
	7	Family	218
	8	Weather	223
	9	Entertaining	229
	10	Business	235
	11	Discussion	241
	12	Training	247

| Answers | 253 |
| Index | 275 |

Introduction

As an intermediate or advanced student of English, you are rapidly expanding your vocabulary. While you are studying, you may also be experiencing some frustration with idiomatic language because it does not follow strict patterns (e.g., the preposition *for* follows the noun *fondness,* but the preposition *of* follows the adjective *fond*). Sometimes the meaning of an idiomatic phrase cannot even be understood from the meaning of its individual words (e.g., the verb phrase *to drop in on someone* has nothing to do with letting something fall). Because rules regarding idiomatic phrases are often vague, practice is the only way to truly master them.

Practice Makes Perfect: Idiomatic English gives you the opportunity to learn more about idiomatic language. You will be introduced to four types of idiomatic phrase: adjective, noun, prepositional, and verb. The book is divided according to phrase type so that you can become familiar with the way parts of speech are combined; however, you will also learn how different phrase types are related. The text includes practice with patterns followed by specific parts of speech, and it also contains activities demonstrating the connection between one type of phrase and another. In addition, units provide ample practice with phrases that lack recognizable patterns. By studying in all these ways, you will be gaining mastery over idiomatic English.

Organization of the Book

The book is divided into four sections: *Adjective Phrases, Noun Phrases, Prepositional Phrases,* and *Verb Phrases.* Within each section, topics are ordered according to the difficulty of their exercises, based on the presence or absence of a pattern in the phrases. However, you can study them in any sequence, depending on your needs. Each unit is organized in the following manner.

- **List of phrases** Phrases are listed alphabetically. Definitions are included when the meaning of a phrase may not be easily understood.

- **Recognition exercises** These exercises give you the opportunity to demonstrate knowledge of the idiomatic phrase's meaning.

- **Pattern exercises** These exercises require you to use a pattern to change a word from one part of speech to another (e.g., from a verb to a noun). However, in the Prepositional Phrases section, practice focuses on the various forms the object can take following multiword prepositions.

- **Sentence formation** The purpose of this activity is to give you practice in placing specific parts of speech or phrases in various types of sentences.

- **Task** The final exercise of each unit asks you to use your knowledge in a specific, real-life situation.

- **Answers** The answers to the exercises are listed in the back of the book.

- **Index** All phrases used in this book are listed alphabetically in the index.

Organization of Each Section

A. Adjective Phrases

Adjective phrases within each unit are listed alphabetically. The adjective appears first, followed by the most commonly used preposition and by an object form (e.g., *someone* or *something*). The adjective phrases chosen for each unit all refer to a specific context (e.g., school), concept (e.g., connections), or emotion (e.g., enchantment). Adjective phrases that are related in some way are listed together.

B. Noun Phrases

In the noun phrases selected for each unit, the noun appears first, followed by the most commonly used preposition and by an object form (e.g., *someone* or *something*). The noun phrases chosen for each unit all refer to a specific context (e.g., education) or concept (e.g., harm and safety). Noun phrases that are related in some way are listed together.

C. Prepositional Phrases

Units C1 through C8 cover prepositional phrases that are set idiomatic expressions (e.g., *in time* and *as a result*). Units C9 through C11 present multiword prepositional phrases, whose object form varies (e.g., *in front of someone or something*).

The prepositional phrases chosen for each unit all refer to a specific context (e.g., buying and selling) or concept (e.g., reference). Prepositional phrases that are related in some way are listed together.

D. Verb Phrases

Three types of multiword verb phrases are presented in this section. Units D1 through D4 focus on prepositional verb phrases. In these units, you will learn to combine verbs with the prepositions most commonly accompanying them (e.g., *focus on*). Units D5 through D11 cover phrasal verbs, which consist of **verb + particle** collocations. Unlike the **verb + preposition** combinations in earlier chapters, **verb + particle** collocations possess meanings that cannot be derived easily from the meaning of the words when they are divided up (e.g., *divide up*). If you have studied phrasal verbs before, you may be familiar with other labels for **particle**. Although "adverb" and "preposition" are sometimes used, **particle** is used here because the words it refers to are distinct from prepositions and other adverbs. Unit D12 deals with **phrasal-prepositional verbs**, which are **verb + particle + preposition** collocations (e.g., *find out about*).

Verb phrases in each unit all refer to a specific context and are listed alphabetically. The verb appears first, followed by the most commonly used preposition or particle. If the verb phrase requires an object, a pronoun will be listed (e.g., *someone* or *something*). In Units D5 through D12, definitions are given for each verb phrase, as the meaning may not be immediately apparent. In addition, each phrasal verb is identified in one of the following ways: **I** = Intransitive, **T-Sep** = Transitive (the verb and particle may be *separated*), **T-Sep (OB)** = the separation is *obligatory*, or **T-Insep** = Transitive (the verb and particle are *inseparable*).

A

Adjective Phrases

Adjective phrases are listed alphabetically. The adjective appears first, followed by the most commonly used preposition and by an object form (e.g., *someone* or *something*). The adjective phrases chosen for each unit all refer to a specific context (e.g., school), concept (e.g., connections), or emotion (e.g., enchantment). Individual adjective phrases that are related in some way are listed together.

Unit A1: Enchantment

amazed by someone or something
  I was amazed by the young athlete.
  We were amazed by her artwork.

amused by something
  I was amused by his remarks.
  We weren't amused by the joke.

beguiled by someone or something
  Antony was beguiled by Cleopatra.
  We were beguiled by the exotic atmosphere.

bewitched by someone or something
  Her fiancé was bewitched by her eyes.
  She was bewitched by her new neighbor.

captivated by someone or something
  We were captivated by his intelligent conversation.
  The audience was captivated by the performance.

charmed by someone or something
  I was charmed by his smile.
  He was charmed by his friend's sister.

enchanted by someone or something
  We were enchanted by the music.
  She was enchanted by the man she met last night.

enthralled by someone or something
  The tourists were enthralled by the landscape.
  The moviegoers were enthralled by the opening scene.

entranced by someone or something
  The students were entranced by the poet.
  We were entranced by his bizzare story.

fascinated by someone or something
  They were fascinated by the intricate dancing.
  Weren't you fascinated by the early explorers?

Exercise 1a

Fill in the blanks below with the correct participles.

> amazed
> amused
> beguiled
> bewitched
> captivated
> charmed
> enchanted

Example: The book critic was <u>enthralled</u> by the novel's plot.

1. They were _____beguiled_____ by the evening light.

2. We were _____charmed_____ by the three tenors.

3. The pioneers were _____amazed_____ by the fertility of the soil.

4. The children were _____amused_____ by the clown's expressions.

5. You were _____captivated_____ by the beautiful flowers in the garden.

6. I was _____bewitched_____ by your glance.

7. He was _____enchanted_____ by her grace and beauty.

Exercise 1b

Which preposition follows the participle in every sentence?

Exercise 2a

Read the first sentence; then complete the second sentence with an idiomatic phrase.

Example: His odd behavior didn't amuse us.
We weren't <u>amused by his odd behavior.</u>

1. Their success amazed us.

   We were <u>amazed by their success</u>.

2. The soundtrack captivated the moviegoers.

   The moviegoers were <u>captivated by the soundtrack</u>.

3. His soft voice bewitched her.

   She was <u>bewitched by his soft voice</u>.

4. Martin's athletic ability fascinated everyone in school.

   Everyone in school was <u>fascinated by Martin's athletic ability</u>.

5. The color of the sunset entranced the couple.

   The couple was <u>entranced by the color of the sunset</u>.

6. The young boy charmed his teacher.

   The teacher was <u>was charmed by the young boy</u>.

7. My friend's sister beguiled me.

   I was <u>beguiled by my friend's sister</u>.

Exercise 2b

When participles refer to emotions, such as those above, which preposition is commonly used? By

often referred as the "passive voice"

Exercise 3a

Read the first sentence; then complete the second sentence with an idiomatic phrase. Hint: To begin the phrase, change the *-ing* participle of the first sentence to a past participle.

Example: We found the desert isle enchanting.
               We were <u>enchanted by the desert isle.</u>

1. The symphony's performance of Beethoven's Fifth was enthralling.

   We were _____.

2. I thought the book was quite amusing.

   I was quite _____.

3. Her smile was beguiling.

   He was _____.

4. We thought the band was amazing.

   We were _____.

5. Our guide was extremely charming.

   We were extremely _____.

6. They found the small cottage enchanting.

   They were _____.

7. I think his paintings are fascinating.

   I am _____.

Exercise 3b

Is the past participle (*-ed* form) or the present participle (*-ing* form) used to refer to the experiencer?

Is the past participle (*-ed* form) or the present participle (*-ing* form) used to refer to the cause of the experience?

Exercise 4

Read the first question; then write a second question with an idiomatic phrase.

Example: Did Marilyn bewitch you?
<u>Were you bewitched by Marilyn?</u>

1. Did the speech captivate the audience?

   _____

2. Did Segovia enthrall the young musicians?

   _____

3. Did his personality entrance you?

   _____

4. Did the novel fascinate you?

   _____

5. Didn't his memory amaze you?

   _____

6. Didn't her conversation amuse you?

   _____

7. Didn't the welcome gift charm the guests?

   _____

8. Didn't the entire evening enchant you?

   _____

Exercise 5

Read the movie review from the magazine *Movies Now;* then answer the questions about it.

> **Loose Strings** ★★★★
>
> Moviegoers looking for enchantment must see *Loose Strings,* a film about two sisters who are charmed by the same man but for different reasons. Jenny is beguiled by Gene's music. They meet in the community orchestra when Gene captivates the audience with his solo performance. Ironically, Julie doesn't like music much at all. When she first meets Gene, they are at the zoo watching otters. Both are amused by the playfulness of the animals. Gene finds the two women fascinating and thinks he is in love with both. The plot unfolds cleverly; if you go to this movie, you will be bewitched by the way three loose strings are pulled together.

Example: What movie will readers of *Movies Now* be enchanted by?
<u>They will be enchanted by *Loose Strings.*</u>

1. Who are Jenny and Julie charmed by?

   _____

2. What is Jenny beguiled by?

   _____

3. Who is captivated by Gene's solo performance?

   _____

4. What are both Gene and Julie amused by?

   _____

5. Who is Gene fascinated by?

   _____

6. What will moviegoers be bewitched by?

   _____

Unit A2: Satisfaction

(un)comfortable with someone or something
> Are you comfortable with the decision?
> I don't feel comfortable with the new manager.

content with something
> We're content with our small apartment.
> Mr. Johnson was content with our first draft.

delighted with something
> We were delighted with her recovery.
> They were delighted with their room.

disappointed in someone or something
> The sports fans were disappointed in the game.
> You seemed disappointed in us.

discontented with someone or something
> Are you discontented with your life?
> Dr. Elwin is discontented with the new nurse.

(un)happy about something
> I'm happy about our decision to move.
> They were unhappy about the change.

okay with someone or something (informal)
> Is the plan okay with you?
> I'm okay with sending the report tomorrow.

(dis)pleased with something or someone
> We were displeased with their attitude.
> Are you pleased with the results of the election?

(dis)satisfied with something or someone
> The guests were dissatisfied with the arrangements.
> We hope that you are satisfied with your new blender.

uneasy about something
> They feel uneasy about the merger.
> I was uneasy about going to the board meeting.

Exercise 1

Fill in the blanks with the correct adjectives.

Example: They're *pleased* with their son's success.

1. Are you _____ with the service?

2. The staff is _____ about the new regulations.

3. We're _____ in your slow progress.

4. They aren't _____ with the new director's manner.

5. The shoppers are _____ with these new high prices.

> comfortable
> disappointed
> discontented
> satisfied
> uneasy

Exercise 2

Circle the preposition that correctly completes the sentence.

Example: He is satisfied _____ his new car.

    (with)   in   about

1. It's okay _____ me.

    with   in   about

2. The little girl was delighted _____ her new doll.

    with   in   for

3. The students were happy _____ the class cancellation.

    with   in   about

4. I'm content _____ a glass of iced tea and a good book.

    with   in   about

5. The coach was displeased _____ the team's poor performance.

    with   in   for

▌Exercise 3

Read the first sentence; then rewrite it by removing the infinitive (*to* + verb) and adding a preposition.

Example: We're happy to receive the bonus.
                 <u>We're happy with the bonus.</u>

1. We're unhappy to receive the rejection.

   _____

2. We're content to have a week of vacation.

   _____

3. We were delighted to receive the award.

   _____

4. We were disappointed to see his sloppy work.

   _____

5. We were pleased to receive the good news.

   _____

6. We were displeased to hear of his thoughtless actions.

   _____

7. We were satisfied to live a simple life.

   _____

8. We were dissatisfied to receive low overtime pay.

   _____

Exercise 4a

Read the first sentence; then complete the second sentence with an idiomatic phrase.

Example: His contentment with the decision was surprising.
He was <u>content with the decision</u>.

1. Her disappointment in my work was evident in the letter she sent me.

   She was _____.

2. Their memo revealed their uneasiness about the project.

   They were _____.

3. We all knew of the director's displeasure with the new camera.

   The director was _____.

4. We could hear in their laughter the children's satisfaction with their new toys.

   The children were _____.

5. My happiness about my promotion subsided when I heard about your dismissal.

   I was _____.

6. The customer reported her dissatisfaction with the company's service.

   The customer was _____.

7. The boy took delight in his new kite.

   The boy was _____.

Exercise 4b

How does *delighted* differ from the other adjectives used above?

Exercise 5

Complete these questions with the correct prepositions. Then answer the questions, using the words in parentheses.

Example: Which meeting time is she okay <u>with</u>? (a morning meeting)
<u>She is okay with a morning meeting.</u>

1. Which candidate is he comfortable _____? (James Marshik)

   _____

2. Which appliance is she dissatisfied _____? (the microwave oven)

   _____

3. What was the actress uneasy _____? (answering the interviewer's question)

   _____

4. Which job were you most content _____? (my work as a sports writer)

   _____

5. Which room are they displeased _____? (Room 4A)

   _____

6. What is she unhappy _____? (her heavy workload)

   _____

Exercise 6

Your friend hired Cal's Catering for her wedding party. After the party, she filled out a customer service questionnaire. Read her questionnaire and answer the questions about it.

CAL'S CATERING SERVICE

Which parts of our service were you satisfied with?

		Comments
☐	promptness	The florists arrived late.
☒	flowers	The lilies were absolutely beautiful.
☒	music	The Bach cantatas were delightful.
☐	decorations	Some of the wall decorations were tacky.
☒	appetizers	The guests raved about the cheese tarts.
☐	entrée	My mother said her fish was cold.
☒	coffee	Fine
☐	wait service	The waitress serving the champagne seemed impatient.

Example: Why wasn't your friend satisfied with the florists?
<u>She wasn't satisfied with the florists because they arrived late.</u>

1. Which entrée was your friend's mother dissatisfied with?

    _____

2. What music was your friend delighted with?

    _____

3. Which decorations was your friend disappointed in?

    _____

4. Which floral arrangement was your friend pleased with?

    _____

5. Was your friend content with the coffee service?

    _____

6. Which waitress was your friend displeased with?

    _____

Unit A3: Work

absent from something
> He was absent from work today.
> Who was absent from the training class?

(in)competent in something
> He's incompetent in cost analysis.
> The translator is competent in five languages.

dedicated to someone or something
> All the employees were dedicated to their generous employer.
> We are dedicated to the company.

enthusiastic about something
> Tim is enthusiastic about his new job.
> The boss wasn't enthusiastic about my proposal.

(un)impressed with someone or something
> I was impressed with the new equipment.
> The supervisor was unimpressed with the new employee.

(un)necessary for something
> These supplies are unnecessary for the project.
> What skills are necessary for the job?

(un)prepared for something
> Are you prepared for your presentation?
> I'm unprepared for today's meeting.

present at something
> Was the supervisor present at the meeting?
> Joanne was not present at the training session.

(un)qualified for something
> Are you qualified for the position?
> He is unqualified for a job with so much responsibility.

(un)suited to something
> He is unsuited to traveling abroad.
> The new employee is suited to working in customer service.

Exercise 1

Fill in the blanks with the correct adjectives.

Example: Which documents are <u>necessary</u> for the meeting?

1. I want to be _____ for the board meeting.

2. Was anyone _____ from the meeting?

3. We need someone who is _____ in Russian and Chinese.

4. Her assistant was _____ to the project.

5. We are _____ with your credentials.

> absent
> competent
> dedicated
> impressed
> prepared

Exercise 2

Circle the preposition that correctly completes the sentence.

Example: The students weren't prepared _____ class.

    in   of   (for)

1. I am qualified _____ the job you posted.

    with   of   for

2. She was present _____ the grand opening.

    with   of   at

3. We are all enthusiastic _____ the new project.

    at   about   in

4. I am not suited _____ this line of work.

    to   of   with

5. Even in his work, he was dedicated _____ environmental causes.

    at   of   to

Exercise 3

Read the first sentence; then complete the second sentence with an idiomatic phrase.

Example: The director noted his absence from the session.
He was <u>absent from the session</u>.

1. She was praised for her competence in international relations.

   She was _____.

2. The article was about Joe's dedication to helping the homeless.

   Joe was _____.

3. The supervisor noted Ed's presence at every conference.

   Ed was _____.

4. A highly skilled technician is a necessity for this job.

   A highly skilled technician is _____.

5. They made preparations for the closure of the plant.

   They were _____.

6. He doesn't have the qualifications for the position.

   He is _____.

7. The client expressed great enthusiasm for our plan.

   The clients were _____.

8. I explained my many absences from work.

   I explained why I was _____.

Exercise 4

Complete these questions with the correct prepositions. Then answer the
questions, using the words in parentheses.

Example: What position is she suited <u>to</u>? (a receptionist position)
<u>She is suited to a receptionist position.</u>

1. Which candidate was the manager most impressed _____?
   (Mr. Hebert)

   _____

2. Which sessions was she absent _____?
   (the two morning sessions)

   _____

3. What are they competent _____? (botany and math)

   _____

4. Who are they dedicated _____? (their families)

   _____

5. What is this tool necessary _____?
   (repairing the office machines)

   _____

6. What part of the application was she unimpressed _____?
   (the candidate's previous experience)

   _____

Exercise 5

Housekeeping Unlimited is advertising job openings in the local newspaper. Read the advertisement; then answer the questions about it.

> ## HOUSEKEEPING UNLIMITED
> Our business is dedicated to keeping houses, offices, and yards in the community clean.
> We are looking for people to fill the following positions:
> **Electricians**—Experience and recommendations necessary.
> **Groundskeepers**—Must be prepared for heavy work. No special training necessary.
> If you would like to be employed at Housekeeping Unlimited, we would like to hear from you. Call now for an application: **487-8906.**

Example: What is the business dedicated to?
<u>It is dedicated to keeping houses, offices, and yards in the community clean.</u>

1. Are recommendations necessary for all jobs?

    _____

2. Would someone without experience be qualified for the job as electrician?

    _____

3. Would the manager be impressed with an applicant who had no experience as an electrician?

    _____

4. What must applicants for the groundskeeping position be prepared for?

    _____

5. What training is necessary for the position of groundskeeper?

    _____

Unit A4: Connections

akin to something
    Raising dogs is akin to parenting.
    Applying for a job in that company is akin to asking for the moon.

comparable to something
    The work there is comparable to slave labor.
    Their results are comparable to ours.

connected to something
    Was he connected to the organization?
    Their point is connected to another issue.

contingent upon something
    Their studies are contingent upon outside support.
    His acceptance was contingent upon several factors.

dependent on someone or something
    Our budget is dependent on the decisions of the legislators.
    They both were dependent on their grandmother.

independent of someone or something
    Jorge is independent of his parents now.
    The colonies wanted to be independent of England.

related to someone or something
    He is related to a famous writer.
    Our topic is related to yours.

(ir)relevant to something
    Her remarks were irrelevant to the discussion.
    His critique is relevant to our subject.

similar to something
    Their car is similar to ours.
    Is Mars similar to Venus?

tied to something
    Ted is tied to the office until next week.
    We were tied to the children's school schedules.

Exercise 1

Fill in the blanks with the correct adjectives.

Example: I am <u>related</u> to a professional tennis player.

1. The economy is _____ on oil.

2. The information is not _____ to our study.

3. Are you _____ to the Internet?

4. Those decisions were _____ of each other.

5. He is _____ to his work.

connected
dependent
independent
relevant
tied

Exercise 2

Circle the preposition that correctly completes the sentence.

Example: The staff was dependent _____ his expertise.

    of   (on)   to

1. Economic growth is contingent _____ improved incomes.

    of   upon   to

2. Cheating is akin _____ theft.

    of   on   to

3. This new machine is comparable _____ one of Edison's inventions.

    of   on   to

4. His study is not related _____ previous research in that area.

    of   upon   to

5. A tart is similar _____ a pie.

    of   on   to

Exercise 3a

Rewrite the sentence, using an adjective + a preposition.

Example: Jane and Sam are related.
            <u>Jane is related to Sam.</u>

1. Economics and ethics are connected.

   _____

2. Field hockey and ice hockey are similar.

   _____

3. Sanskrit and Latin are related.

   _____

4. His novel and John Updike's are not comparable.

   _____

5. A nectarine and a peach are similar.

   _____

Exercise 3b

Does *akin* follow the pattern above?

Exercise 4

Complete these questions with the correct prepositions.

1. What is your decision contingent _____?

2. Who is he dependent _____?

3. Who is she trying to become independent _____?

4. What are their comments relevant _____?

5. What are you tied _____?

Exercise 5

Read the first sentence; then complete the second sentence with an idiomatic phrase.

Example: Their comparison of Earth to Pluto was farfetched.
              They said Earth was <u>comparable to Pluto</u>.

1. His ties to his family were tenuous.

    He was _____.

2. Her connection to the incident was problematic.

    She was _____.

3. The relation of cancer to smoking is clear.

    Cancer is _____.

4. They described the irrelevance of his testimony to the case.

    His testimony was _____.

5. Their dependence on drugs was unhealthy.

    They were _____.

6. The new music's similarity to classical music is remarkable.

    The new music is _____.

7. Their comparison of the sound of her voice to the sound of a flute was appropriate.

    They said the sound of her voice was _____.

Exercise 6

A crazy professor named Professor Oddball is always making strange connections between one thing and another in his class, "History of Sports." Read the notes his students take; then answer questions about them.

> "Ping pong and soccer are related."
>
> "Football players can be compared to nurses."
>
> "The popularity of sports was contingent upon the invention of the automobile."
>
> "Baseball and volleyball are similar."
>
> "Riding a bike is akin to hitting a golf ball."
>
> "Amateurs depend on their shoes for success."
>
> "Failure is tied to practicing too much."

Example: What does Professor Oddball say ping pong is related to?
<u>Professor Oddball says ping pong is related to soccer.</u>

1. Who does Professor Oddball say football players are comparable to?

   _____

2. What does Professor Oddball say the popularity of sports was contingent upon?

   _____

3. What does Professor Oddball say that baseball is similar to?

   _____

4. What does Professor Oddball say that riding a bike is akin to?

   _____

5. What does Professor Oddball say that amateurs are dependent on for success?

   _____

6. What does Professor Oddball say failure is tied to?

   _____

Unit A5: Turmoil

angry about something
> They are angry about the new schedule.
> The student is angry about her grade.

angry at someone
> Why are you angry at her?
> She's angry at me.

disgusted with something
> I'm disgusted with the service.
> He was disgusted with his son's behavior.

envious of someone or something
> The couple is envious of their new neighbors.
> My friends are envious of my success.

fed up with something (informal)
> Aren't you fed up with his demands?
> They were fed up with the stress of city life, so they moved to the country.

furious with someone or something
> The teacher is furious with her students' lack of effort.
> The coach is furious with the referee.

jealous of someone or something
> She's jealous of her younger sister.
> That writer is jealous of his friend's good fortune.

mad at someone (informal)
> Are you mad at me?
> He's mad at his boss for refusing his request.

sick of something (informal)
> I'm sick of your excuses.
> We're sick of working with them.

tired of something
> I'm tired of your company.
> The students are tired of doing homework.

Exercise 1

Fill in the blanks with the correct adjectives.

Example: The shoppers were <u>sick</u> of the long check-out lines.

1. Why is he _____ of your good luck?

2. He is _____ about the new regulations.

3. They're _____ of your complaints.

4. She's _____ with the traffic delays.

5. Shirley is _____ at her sister.

> angry
>
> disgusted
>
> envious
>
> mad
>
> tired

Exercise 2

Circle the preposition that correctly completes the sentence.

Example: Why are you envious _____ him?

    at   (of)   about

1. You are angry _____ nothing.

    about   of   with

2. The public grew disgusted _____ the transportation strike.

    about   of   with

3. Ronnie was jealous _____ his friends.

    at   of   with

4. The citizens were furious _____ their legislators.

    about   of   with

5. I am fed up _____ the whole thing.

    at   of   with

Exercise 3

Read the first sentence; then complete the second sentence with an idiomatic phrase.

Example: Their anger at the police was frightening.
                They were <u>angry at the police</u>.

1. Her fury with their incompetence was boundless.

    She was _____.

2. The coach doesn't understand Lou's envy of his teammates.

    Lou is _____.

3. Sven's jealousy of his fellow musicians is unreasonable.

    Sven is _____.

4. His anger about the accident finally subsided.

    He was _____.

5. The supervisor's disgust with the incident showed on her face.

    She was _____.

Exercise 4

Complete these questions with the correct prepositions.

Example: Who are you fed up <u>with</u>?

1. Who are they mad _____?

2. What are you angry _____?

3. Who is he jealous _____?

4. Who is she disgusted _____?

5. Who is the CEO furious _____?

▍Exercise 5

You attended a protest on a college campus, but the only person you knew there was your friend. After the protest, you tried to find out who everyone was by asking, "Who was the person who . . . ?" Supply the correct preposition.

Example: Someone was angry <u>at</u> the administration.
<u>Who was the person who was angry at the administration?</u>

1. Someone was angry _____ the tuition hike.

   _____

2. Someone was disgusted _____ the cut in the library budget.

   _____

3. Someone was fed up _____ the poor athletics programs.

   _____

4. Someone was furious _____ the Dean of Student Affairs.

   _____

5. Someone was tired _____ receiving so little financial aid.

   _____

6. Someone was sick _____ the cafeteria food.

   _____

Exercise 6

Ella Landon is outraged about a recent city council decision to sell public park land. Read her letter to the editor in the *Lake City News* and answer the questions about it.

Dear Editor:

We have one of the loveliest towns in the state. In fact, people from other towns are jealous of our beautiful parks. However, if we don't convince our council members to rescind their recent decision, soon **we** will be envious of citizens from Shoreview and Rosemont. I must say I am furious with the decision to sell off East Lake Park to developers.

I'm not a person who gets mad at others easily, but I am extremely angry at the council for not consulting the citizens before making a decision. I am fed up with their arrogance, and I urge all citizens of Lake City who are tired of hasty council decisions to write to the council members.

Sincerely,
Ella Landon

Example: What are people from other towns jealous of?
<u>They are jealous of the beautiful parks in Lake City.</u>

1. Who will the citizens of Lake City be envious of?

   _____

2. What is Ella Landon furious with?

   _____

3. Who does not get mad at others easily?

   _____

4. Who is Ella extremely angry at?

   _____

5. What is Ella fed up with?

   _____

6. According to Ella, who should write to the council members?

   _____

Unit A6: Attraction

attached to someone or something
> Although an adult, she is still attached to her parents.
> He's quite attached to his routine.

attracted to someone or something
> I was attracted to the piano because my grandmother was a concert pianist.
> He was attracted to my roommate.

close to someone
> He's close to his mother.
> As a boy he was close to his grandfather.

devoted to someone or something
> Sam is devoted to environmental causes.
> They are still devoted to each other.

enamored of someone or something
> She's enamored of young movie stars.
> I am enamored of Egyptian history.

engaged to someone
> My sister is engaged to James.
> He's engaged to my sister.

fond of someone or something
> Who isn't fond of chocolate?
> She's very fond of her young nieces.

infatuated with someone
> She was infatuated with the neighbor boy.
> The six-year-old is infatuated with Batman.

married to someone
> I'm married to someone I met at college.
> He's married to my sister.

taken with someone or something
> The president is quite taken with the idea.
> When they first met, she was quite taken with him.

Exercise 1

Fill in the blanks with the correct adjectives.

Example: The twin sisters were <u>close</u> to each other, even as adults.

1. Chris is _____ to his music.

2. The whole staff was _____ of jelly doughnuts.

3. He is _____ to a sports star; their wedding will be in May.

4. I was _____ with my brother's friend for a long time.

5. He is _____ to his childhood sweetheart and has three kids.

> devoted
>
> engaged
>
> fond
>
> infatuated
>
> married

Exercise 2

Circle the preposition that correctly completes the sentence.

Example: Beth is engaged _____ someone she met in Pittsburgh.

  of   (to)   with

1. The supervisor isn't taken _____ your proposal.

  of   to   with

2. The young naturalist was enamored _____ the land.

  of   to   with

3. He was attracted _____ the crime world.

  of   to   with

4. Because she had family there, she was attached _____ the area.

  of   to   with

5. Mr. Carlson is very fond _____ his grandson.

  of   to   with

Exercise 3

A new coworker asks you many questions about the people you work with. Unfortunately, you don't know the answers to them. Complete her questions with the correct prepositions. Then answer her questions, beginning with "I don't know . . . ."

Example: Who was Jay attached <u>to</u> when he was young?
<u>I don't know who he was attached to when he was young.</u>

1. Who is Gloria married _____?

   _____

2. Who are the Thams close _____?

   _____

3. What project is Ted devoted _____?

   _____

4. Who is Kay engaged _____?

   _____

5. What kinds of ideas is our manager taken _____?

   _____

6. What kind of coffee-break treats is the whole staff fond _____?

   _____

Exercise 4

Read the first sentence; then use the adjective in parentheses to write your own sentence.

Example: Susie and Diana were friends and knew each other very well.
(close)
<u>Susie and Diana were close to each other.</u>

1. John doesn't like ice cream. (fond)

   _____

2. Atsuko is not planning to marry James. (engaged)

   _____

3. Lee's wife's name is Julia. (married)

   _____

4. Clara does everything she can for the equal rights movement. (devoted)

   _____

5. She really likes her high school friends. (very attached)

   _____

6. Even though she was good looking, he didn't like her. (attracted)

   _____

7. My aunt likes roses very much. (enamored)

   _____

8. Arnie likes this place a lot. (quite taken)

   _____

Exercise 5

Your friend Sherry has decided to run a personal ad. Read the questionnaire she filled out; then answer the questions about it.

PRIVATE EYE PERSONALS

Have you ever been married to anyone? _____ No _____

Have you ever been engaged to anyone? _____ Yes (when I was 18) _____

What type of person would you like to be close to?
_____ Someone who likes to travel _____

What type of person are you attracted to?
_____ Someone who is interested in foreign languages and cultures _____

What things in your life are you devoted to?
_____ I am devoted to my job as a mapmaker. _____

What types of food are you fond of?
_____ All types of ethnic food; not hamburgers and french fries _____

What movies have you been quite taken with?
_____ Dances with Wolves, Black Robe _____

Example: Has Sherry ever been married to anyone?
<u>No, she has never been married to anyone.</u>

1. When was Sherry engaged to someone?

   _____

2. Who would Sherry like to be close to?

   _____

3. Is Sherry attracted to someone who likes to watch TV?

   _____

4. What is Sherry devoted to?

   _____

5. Is Sherry fond of hamburgers and french fries?

   _____

6. What movies was Sherry quite taken with?

   _____

Unit A7: School

(un)accustomed to someone or something
> New students must get accustomed to their instructors.
> College freshman are unaccustomed to so much homework.

(un)aware of something
> I wasn't aware of that.
> He was unaware of the change in school policy.

bored with something
> They were bored with the story.
> I was bored with the lecture.

(in)capable of something
> The second-grader was capable of reading beyond her grade level.
> Are the children incapable of cleaning up?

engaged in something
> The students were engaged in a lively discussion.
> The children were engaged in the activity.

open to something
> The teacher was open to suggestions for improving the class.
> Some students are not open to discussing political issues.

proud of something
> You all can be proud of the progress you have made.
> Kelly was proud of her success in the class.

responsible for something
> You are responsible for turning your work in on time.
> The teacher is responsible for returning your work promptly.

(in)tolerant of something
> We were tolerant of different opinions.
> The teacher was intolerant of our questions.

used to someone or something
> The international students were not used to one another.
> Every quarter the students had to get used to new schedules.

Exercise 1

Fill in the blanks with the correct adjectives.

Example: We were <u>tolerant</u> of other people's opinions.

1. My son is _____ with school.

2. She was so _____ in her work that she didn't hear us.

3. Alice was _____ to living in a dorm.

4. The boy was _____ of his achievement.

5. Each student is _____ for doing part of the project.

> bored
>
> engaged
>
> proud
>
> responsible
>
> unaccustomed

Exercise 2

Circle the preposition that correctly completes the sentence.

Example: The children were quickly bored _____ the activity.

      in   of   (with)

1. They were tolerant _____ each other's bad habits.

      with   of   for

2. He wasn't aware _____ his own accent.

      with   of   in

3. She wasn't capable _____ passing the swimming test.

      to   of   for

4. We were open _____ new ideas.

      to   of   with

5. Laura is not used _____ her new teacher yet.

      in   of   to

Exercise 3

Rewrite each sentence, using the adjective in parentheses. Hint: The object following the preposition will be the *-ing* form of the verb from the first sentence.

Example: Students do math drills. (bored)
<u>Students are bored with doing math drills.</u>

1. Most children share lockers. (accustomed)

   _____

2. Students learn new things. (open)

   _____

3. Students get good grades. (proud)

   _____

4. Students lead discussions. (responsible)

   _____

5. Students help others. (used)

   _____

6. The librarian disturbed the students. (unaware)

   _____

7. Some preschoolers sit still. (incapable)

   _____

8. By second grade, students listen to long stories. (capable)

   _____

Exercise 4

You attended your first day of college classes, but the only person you knew there was your friend. Over dinner, you tried to find out who everyone was by asking, "Who was the person who . . . ?" Supply the correct preposition.

Example: Someone was unaccustomed <u>to</u> participating in class discussions. <u>Who was the person who was unaccustomed to participating in class discussions?</u>

1. Someone was bored _____ the history lecture.

   _____

2. Someone was incapable _____ being quiet during class.

   _____

3. Someone was engaged _____ a loud conversation with the biology professor.

   _____

4. Someone was responsible _____ giving new students a campus tour.

   _____

5. Someone was unaware _____ the registration deadline.

   _____

6. Someone was used _____ living in dormitories.

   _____

Exercise 5

This poster appeared on many college bulletin boards. Read the poster; then answer the questions about it.

Have Fun! Join the Outing Club!

- Are you unaccustomed to a lonely college life? If you are, join us for our opening picnic.
- Are you bored with college life? If you are, hike with us up the Ridge Trail.
- Are you incapable of running a mile? If you are, get in shape with us.
- Are you open to adventure? If you are, camp with us at the summit of Mt. Hart.
- Are you used to walking, biking, and skiing long distances? If you are, join us.
- Are you aware of the fun you could have? If you aren't, call Jason (ext. 356) to find out more.

OUTING CLUB MEMBERS ARE PROUD OF HAVING FUN!

Example: What should students do if they are unaccustomed to a lonely college life?
<u>If they are unaccustomed to a lonely college life, they should join the Outing Club for the opening picnic.</u>

1. Who should hike up the Ridge Trail with the Outing Club?

   _____

2. Who should get in shape with the Outing Club?

   _____

3. What should a student who is open to adventure do?

   _____

4. What are many of the students who join the Outing Club used to?

   _____

5. If students are unaware of the fun they could have, what should they do?

   _____

6. What are Outing Club members proud of?

   _____

Unit A8: Talent

accomplished at something

Although young, she is quite accomplished at writing poetry.
Al was accomplished at composing music for children.

blessed with something

My sister was blessed with the ability to draw.
She was also blessed with a beautiful voice.

confident of something

He was confident of his success.
The team is confident of victory.

endowed with something

They were both endowed with keen intellect.
You were endowed with a good sense of humor.

expert at something

My nephew is expert at solving math problems.
The new employee was expert at strategizing.

gifted with something

Nort was gifted with unbelievable accounting skills.
Larry was gifted with an extraordinary imagination.

good at something

She's good at cards.
The kids are good at checkers.

sure of someone or something

He didn't seem sure of himself today.
She was so sure of her success that her failure surprised her.

talented at something

Mom's friend is talented at gardening.
He is talented at raising money.

unrivaled in something

The Red Sox are unrivaled in pitching talent.
The young tennis player is unrivaled in tenacity.

Exercise 1

Fill in the blanks with the correct adjectives.

Example: Both girls were <u>endowed</u> with talent.

1. He became quite _____ at learning
    languages.

2. The athlete was _____ with speed.

3. Jacob is _____ of his abilities.

4. Grandpa was _____ at predicting
    storms.

5. The soccer team was _____
    in young talent until this year.

blessed
confident
expert
talented
unrivaled

Exercise 2

Circle the preposition that correctly completes the sentence.

Example: My daughter was confident _____ her ability to make the team.

  at   in   (of)

1. Sally was endowed _____ a quick mind.

  at   of   with

2. The applicant was sure _____ his qualifications.

  in   of   with

3. Ethan is accomplished _____ playing the piano.

  in   of   at

4. My friend is really good _____ raising animals.

  at   of   with

5. The musician said he was gifted _____ long fingers.

  in   of   with

Exercise 3a

Your friend Carlo is both talented and confident. Use the adjective in parentheses to write statements about him. Hint: The object following the preposition will be the *-ing* form of the verb from the first sentence.

Example: Carlo tells funny stories. (accomplished)
               Carlo is accomplished at telling funny stories.

1. Carlo can write catchy tunes. (talented)

   _____

2. Carlo can entertain all types of people. (good)

   _____

3. Carlo gets lots of laughs. (sure)

   _____

4. Carlo is able to make people happy. (confident)

   _____

Exercise 3b

Use the sentences above to tell why Carlo was hired as a comedian. Use the pattern "so + adjective *that he was hired immediately.*"

Example: Carlo was so accomplished at telling funny stories that he was hired immediately.

1. _____

2. _____

3. _____

4. _____

Exercise 4a

You and your friends are baffled by Lin's lack of talent. Use negative yes/no rhetorical questions with idiomatic phrases to indicate how you might express your puzzlement.

Example: Lin isn't talented.
              <u>Isn't Lin talented at anything?</u>

1. Lin isn't an expert.

   _____

2. Lin isn't good at anything.

   _____

3. Lin wasn't gifted.

   _____

4. Lin wasn't blessed.

   _____

5. Lin isn't confident.

   _____

Exercise 4b

You want to help Lin gain self-esteem by discovering what he is good at. Change the questions above to complete the *wh-* questions you might ask yourself.

Example: What is <u>Lin talented at</u>?

1. What is _____?

2. What is _____?

3. What was _____?

4. What was _____?

5. What is _____?

Exercise 5

The following article appeared on your local sports page yesterday. Read the article; then answer the questions about it.

Blasters Are Back

The Sandblasters volleyball team will be playing tonight at the Center. Coach Allen says the team has been blessed with good health this week so they are sure of victory over the Waves.

This year the Blasters have been unrivaled in spiking talent. However, until today, the coach was worried that Mary Andrews, expert at setting up spiking opportunities, would not be able to play. Although there are other players good at setting, with Andrews out, the team wouldn't be so confident of winning. Andrews says she feels strong and sure of her ability to perform tonight.

Example: What have the Sandblasters been blessed with?
<u>They have been blessed with good health.</u>

1. What is Coach Allen sure of?

    _____

2. What have the Blasters been unrivaled in this year?

    _____

3. Who is expert at setting up spiking opportunities?

    _____

4. Are there players besides Andrews who are good at setting?

    _____

5. Without Andrews, would the team be confident of winning?

    _____

6. What is Andrews sure of?

    _____

Unit A9: Kindness

appreciative of something

They have been very appreciative of our support.

I am very appreciative of your recommendation.

good of someone

It was good of you to help the elderly do their shopping.

That was good of you.

grateful to someone / for something

We are grateful to you for your help.

I am very grateful for your assistance in this matter.

indebted to someone (for something)

I'm indebted to all those who helped me.

She is indebted to her teachers for their constant encouragement.

kind of someone

It was kind of you to buy all our tickets.

That was kind of you.

nice of someone

It was nice of you to remember my birthday.

That was nice of you.

sensitive to something

The nurse was sensitive to my fear of needles.

The teacher was sensitive to our needs.

sorry for something

I'm sorry for the interruption.

He's sorry for disturbing you.

thankful for something

We are thankful for your many kindnesses.

They are very thankful for his assistance.

thoughtful of someone

It was thoughtful of you to send flowers.

That was thoughtful of you.

Exercise 1

Fill in the blanks with the correct adjectives.

Example: We were <u>appreciative</u> of the donor's generosity.

1. I am _____ to them for their valuable suggestions.

2. He was _____ for his rude behavior.

3. It was _____ of you to plan his retirement party.

4. The counselor was _____ to her patient's distress.

5. Our family is _____ for your kindness.

> grateful
> sensitive
> sorry
> thankful
> thoughtful

Exercise 2

Circle the preposition that correctly completes the sentence.

Example: It was good _____ you to call.

      for   (of)   to

1. It was nice _____ you to help me clean up.

      for   of   to

2. He's indebted _____ his older sister for paying his tuition.

      for   of   to

3. The client was grateful _____ the advice.

      for   of   to

4. It was kind _____ you to send the family a sympathy card.

      for   of   to

5. The museum curator was appreciative _____ our donation.

      for   of   to

Exercise 3

Someone is being kind. You recognize his or her kindness with the following phrase: "It was _____ of you _____."
Use an adjective from the box and an infinitive phrase.

Example: Your sister took the neighbor kids to the swimming pool.
<u>It was nice of you to take the neighbor kids to the swimming pool.</u>

good

nice

kind

thoughtful

1. Your friend invited you to dinner.

_____

2. Your coworker helped you finish your work.

_____

3. Your aunt and uncle sent you flowers when you were sick.

_____

4. Your cousin took Grandma to the clinic.

_____

5. Your supervisor allowed you to have an extra day of vacation.

_____

6. Your neighbor took care of your cat while you were away.

_____

7. Your friend cleaned Mr. Fowler's house for him.

_____

8. Your mother watered your plants for you while you were away.

_____

Exercise 4

Change these sentences into questions. The *wh-* word replaces the underlined words.

Example: The student said he was appreciative of <u>the special lesson</u>.
What <u>did the student say he was appreciative of</u>?

1. They were indebted to the staff for <u>their assistance</u>.

   What _____?

2. She was sorry for <u>arriving late</u>.

   What _____?

3. The farmers were thankful for <u>the good growing season</u>.

   What _____?

4. Ms. Brady is sensitive to <u>the feelings of small children</u>.

   What _____?

5. The patient was appreciative of <u>the constant attention</u>.

   What _____?

6. It was nice of him to <u>cook dinner for us</u>.

   What _____?

7. It was good of Grandpa to <u>take Erik to the museum</u>.

   What _____?

8. It was thoughtful of the teacher to <u>give us extra help</u>.

   What _____?

Exercise 5

It's Secretary's Day. Everyone in the office signs a thank-you card for Sara. Read the card; then answer the questions about it.

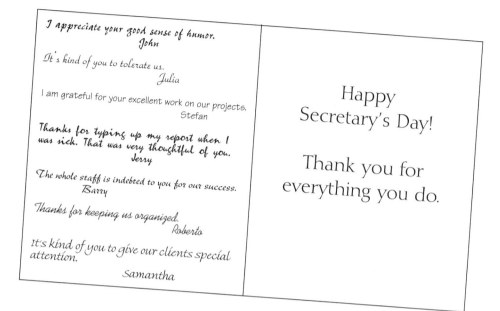

Example: Who is appreciative of Sara's good humor?
<u>John is appreciative of Sara's good humor.</u>

1. Who is thankful for Sara's organizational skills?

   _____

2. Who is the staff indebted to for their success?

   _____

3. Who is grateful for Sara's work on projects?

   _____

4. Who is appreciative of Sara's thoughtfulness?

   _____

5. What does Samantha think it's kind of Sara to do?

   _____

6. Who is appreciative of Sara's tolerance?

   _____

Unit A10: Travel

adjacent to something
> Our room was adjacent to theirs.
> The dining room is adjacent to the lobby.

bound for somewhere
> They are bound for Alaska.
> This team is bound for Salzburg.

different from something
> Their alphabet is different from ours.
> Your driving laws are different from theirs.

excited about something
> The students are excited about their upcoming trip.
> They were excited about going shopping.

(un)familiar with something
> The tour guide is very familiar with this region.
> I was unfamiliar with Chinese art.

famous for something
> Fenway Park, located near Kenmore Square, is famous for its hotdogs.
> Boston is famous for its historical buildings.

far from somewhere
> We are far from home.
> Are we far from our hotel?

homesick for something
> I'm homesick for Mom's cooking.
> She's homesick for familiar sights and sounds.

ready for something
> Are you ready for the trip?
> He's ready for anything.

(un)suitable for something
> Those shoes are unsuitable for walking in all day.
> This coat is suitable for all types of weather.

Exercise 1

Fill in the blanks with the correct adjectives.

Example: Tomorrow I'm <u>bound</u> for home.

1. The bus depot is _____ to the train station.

2. Norway is _____ for its fjords.

3. Are we _____ from our destination?

4. Bobby is _____ about going to Disneyland.

5. Your clothes are _____ for that climate.

> adjacent
>
> excited
>
> famous
>
> far
>
> unsuitable

Exercise 2

Circle the preposition that correctly completes the sentence.

Example: She's homesick _____ the bright lights of Broadway.

     (for)   of   to

1. I'm unfamiliar _____ the customs of your country.

     for   with   to

2. Are they ready _____ the bus?

     for   from   to

3. Their lifestyle is very different _____ ours.

     for   from   with

4. He always gets very excited _____ going to new places.

     for   about   to

5. This train is bound _____ Chicago.

     for   about   to

Exercise 3

Rewrite the sentences below, deleting the relative pronoun and the *be* verb. Supply the correct prepositions.

Example: I was the only person who was homesick <u>for</u> my country.
<u>I was the only person homesick for my country.</u>

1. The children stayed in a room that was adjacent _____ ours.

   _____

2. We were the only tourists who were unfamiliar _____ Setswana.

   _____

3. The city that is famous _____ skyscrapers is New York.

   _____

4. You should buy shoes that are suitable _____ walking.

   _____

5. Tom is the only student who is ready _____ today's tour.

   _____

6. There are many students who are excited _____ the trip.

   _____

Exercise 4

Complete these questions with the correct prepositions. Then answer the questions, using the words in parentheses.

Example: Which areas of the country are you familiar <u>with</u>?
(the coastal regions)
<u>I am familiar with the coastal regions.</u>

1. What is she homesick _____? (familiar faces and places)

_____

2. Where are they bound _____? (the Everglades)

_____

3. What is New Orleans famous _____? (Mardi Gras)

_____

4. What are the children excited _____? (their trip to Yellowstone)

_____

5. What building is the post office adjacent _____?
(the public library)

_____

6. What type of clothing is suitable _____ the occasion?
(formal)

_____

Exercise 5

You have received a brochure in the mail from a resort in the San Juan Islands. Read the brochure; then answer the questions about it.

THE COVE RESORT

Are you ready for something different? Visit the San Juans and stay with us. We are far from crowds but not far from fun. Our resort is adjacent to the San Juan Marina, where you can rent sailboats, canoes, and kayaks. There's something for everyone to get excited about.

COME TO THE COVE RESORT

We're famous for peace, quiet, and fun. Make your reservations now. Don't be bound to your job; be bound for the San Juans.

Example: According to the brochure, who should stay at the Cove Resort? <u>Someone ready for something different should stay at the Cove Resort.</u>

1. What is the Cove Resort far from?

   _____

2. What is the Cove Resort not far from?

   _____

3. What is the Cove Resort adjacent to?

   _____

4. Will everyone in your group find something to do?

   _____

5. What is the Cove Resort famous for?

   _____

6. Instead of being bound to a job, where should everyone be bound for?

   _____

Unit A11: Trouble

(un)afraid of someone or something

    The little girl was unafraid of the big dog.

    Aren't you afraid of her?

anxious about something

    The prime minister was anxious about the country's unstable situation.

    They are anxious about the test results.

apprehensive about something

    They were apprehensive about the future.

    We were apprehensive about the exam.

(un)ashamed of someone or something

    He was ashamed of himself for shouting.

    I am unashamed of my response.

confused about something

    Sandra is confused about her responsibilities.

    We were both confused about the time.

fearful of something

    They were fearful of failure.

    The investors were fearful of a stock market crash.

nervous about something

    Are you nervous about your doctor's appointment?

    He was nervous about the interview.

suspicious of someone or something

    He was suspicious of meeting me at such a late hour.

    We were suspicious of his motives.

troubled about something

    She was troubled about her relationship with Bob.

    The parents were troubled about their daughter's rude behavior.

upset about something

    The little boy was upset about the move.

    I was upset about my best friend's accident.

Exercise 1

Fill in the blanks with the correct adjectives.

Example: She was not <u>ashamed</u> of her actions.

1. The students were _____ about the assignment.
   They didn't know what to do.

2. He is very _____ of Roberta because
   of her deviousness.

3. The fan was so _____ about the
   game's final inning that he was biting his nails.

4. Scott was _____ about his parents'
   divorce.

5. She was _____ of losing her friends.

afraid

confused

nervous

suspicious

upset

Exercise 2

Circle the preposition that correctly completes the sentence.

Example: You are upset _____ nothing.

     of   (about)

1. She was ashamed _____ her family.

     of   about

2. He was fearful _____ the consequences.

     of   about

3. Ms. Ristine is anxious _____ her new job.

     of   about

4. The lawyer was apprehensive _____ the trial.

     of   about

5. The politician was unafraid _____ the public's reaction.

     of   about

Exercise 3

Rewrite the sentences below, deleting *because*, the noun or pronoun, and the *be* verb. Supply the correct prepositions.

Example: Because he was troubled <u>about</u> his daughter's slow progress, he made an appointment to see the principal.
<u>Troubled about his daughter's slow progress, he made an</u>
<u>appointment to see the principal.</u>

1. Because they were suspicious _____ the strange-looking boy, they called the police.

    _____

2. Because the hiker was confused _____ her location, she took out her compass and map.

    _____

3. Because she was nervous _____ her wedding, she decided to call her mother.

    _____

4. Because he was ashamed _____ his outburst, he planned to write a letter of apology.

    _____

5. Because they were afraid _____ walking at night, they decided to call a taxi.

    _____

6. Because the student was anxious _____ her freshman year, she planned to visit the campus during the summer.

    _____

Exercise 4

Complete these questions with the correct prepositions. Then answer the questions, using the words in parentheses.

Example: What are the students confused _____?
(the directions to the first exercise)
<u>They are confused about the directions to the first exercise.</u>

1. What is the diplomat apprehensive _____? (her meeting tomorrow)

   _____

2. Who are you suspicious _____? (the butler)

   _____

3. What is your daughter upset _____? (her sick puppy)

   _____

4. What is Mr. Hanson troubled _____?
   (his mother's failing health)

   _____

5. What is she anxious _____? (the audit)

   _____

6. What are the parents fearful _____?
   (their son's involvement in a gang)

   _____

Exercise 5

At a meeting of the city council, members discussed recent events. Read the transcript of their meeting; then answer the questions about it.

MR. LEE: I'm nervous about the mayor's decision to remove building restrictions.

MS. HEASER: Why are you upset about that?

MR. LEE: I'm afraid of abuses. Someone could build a liquor store right next to a school.

DR. HARMON: I'm a little suspicious of the mayor's decision, too. Why didn't he consult the council first? He seems to be confused about the procedures we usually follow.

MS. HEASER: I don't think we have anything to be anxious about. The mayor is an honest man.

DR. HARMON: Well, I'm apprehensive about the ramifications of the mayor's decision and would like us to write a letter to him.

Example: What is Mr. Lee nervous about?
<u>He's nervous about the mayor's decision to remove building restrictions.</u>

1. Is Ms. Heaser upset about the mayor's decision?

   _____

2. What is Mr. Lee afraid of?

   _____

3. What is Dr. Harmon suspicious of?

   _____

4. What might the mayor be confused about?

   _____

5. What does Ms. Heaser think about the situation?

   _____

6. What is Dr. Harmon apprehensive about?

   _____

B

Noun Phrases

Noun phrases are listed alphabetically. The noun appears first, followed by the most commonly used prepositions and by an object form (e.g., *someone* or *something*). The noun phrases chosen for each unit all refer to a specific context (e.g., education) or concept (e.g., harm and safety). Noun phrases that are related in some way are listed together.

Unit B1: Family Life

care of someone

> The care of the child is the parents' responsibility.
> I took care of my little brother after school.

dependence on someone

> They are young, so their dependence on their parents is great.
> My grandmother's dependence on us grew each year.

habit of doing something

> My brother had a bad habit of snapping his gum.
> My sister has a habit of waking me up when she wakes up.

help with something

> I always needed help with spelling words.
> My brother never needed help with his homework.

influence on someone

> Older siblings often have influence on younger brothers and sisters.
> Parents can have a great influence on their children.

love for someone

> His love for his children was enormous.
> No one doubted her love for her husband.

(im)patience with someone

> I learned to play tennis because my brother had patience with me.
> My father's impatience with me showed in his voice.

photograph/picture of someone or something

> I have a picture of my daughter in my wallet.
> She has a photograph of her family on the wall.

quarrel with someone

> His quarrels with his parents never lasted long.
> My quarrel with my brother ended in silence.

relationship between persons

> There was a close relationship between my mother and her sister.
> The relationship between my sisters was strained.

Exercise 1

Fill in the blanks below with the correct noun.

Example: Children should take <u>care</u> of their pets.

1. One's _____ on parents lasts a long time.

2. What was the _____ with your brother about?

3. Please have _____ with me.

4. Who had the most _____ on you when you were young?

5. Dad wanted _____ with chores.

help

influence

dependence

patience

quarrel

Exercise 2

Circle the preposition that correctly completes the sentence.

Example: I have a bad habit _____ biting my nails.

    on   in   (of)

1. She talked about her love _____ her children.

    for   in   with

2. We were concerned about the care _____ my grandmother.

    on   in   of

3. My parents' patience _____ their seven children was incredible.

    with   on   of

4. May I see a picture _____ our family?

    on   in   of

Exercise 3

Read the first sentence; then complete the second sentence with a
noun + preposition. Hint: If the verb is followed by a preposition, use that
preposition. If the verb is not followed by a preposition, use *of*.

Example: We depended on my father.
Our <u>dependence on</u> my father never bothered him.

1. I quarreled with my sister last night.

   My _____ my sister lasted all evening.

2. He photographed my newborn.

   His _____ my newborn won an award.

3. She helped with the work.

   I asked her for _____ the work.

4. When we are young, we depend on our parents.

   Children's _____ their parents is great.

Exercise 4

Read the first sentence; then complete the second sentence with an
idiomatic noun phrase.

Example: I photographed my two sons.
I took a <u>photograph of my two sons</u>.

1. My sister depended on me.

   My sister's _____ made me feel important.

2. The two boys always quarreled with each other.

   Their _____ were not serious.

3. Did someone help you with your project?

   Did you receive _____?

Exercise 5

Read the first sentence; then complete the second sentence with a preposition + gerund.

Example: She always teases her little brother.
She has a bad habit <u>of teasing</u> her little brother.

1. They depend on their parents for everything.

   They have a habit _____ on their parents for everything.

2. My brother complains about every meal.

   My brother has a bad habit _____ about every meal.

3. I always quarrel with my cousins.

   I have a bad habit _____ with my cousins.

4. My mother always does two things at once.

   My mother has a habit _____ two things at once.

5. You always deny my requests.

   You have a habit _____ my requests.

Exercise 6

Complete these questions with the correct preposition.

Example: Who is the photograph <u>of</u> ?

1. Who was your quarrel _____?

2. What do you need help _____?

3. Who did you take care _____?

4. Who did he have influence _____?

5. Who did you have to have patience _____?

Exercise 7

Read the excerpts from Lila's diary. Answer the questions about them in full sentences.

Example: Who did Lenny have a great influence on?
<u>Lenny had a great influence on Lila.</u>

1. Who did Lila take pictures of?

   _____

2. What did Lila appreciate?

   _____

3. What did Eva ask Lila for help with?

   _____

4. What was remarkable?

   _____

5. What was the relationship between Lila's parents like?

   _____

6. Who had a habit of asking for help with everything?

   _____

My older brother, Lenny, had a great influence on me.

My older sister, Eva, asked me for help with everything.

The relationship between my parents was loving.

I appreciated my grandfather's patience with me.

My parents' love for their children was remarkable.

I took many pictures of Lenny and Eva.

Unit B2: Entertainment

book about someone or something
> I'm looking for a book about the Civil War.
> Do you have any books about Ronald Reagan?

cancellation of something
> We were disappointed about the cancellation of the concert.
> The cancellation of the series was due to the star's sudden death.

concert of something
> We went to a concert of baroque music.
> The concert of folk music was well attended.

exhibit of something
> There was an exhibit of black-and-white photographs.
> The exhibit of Andrew Wyeth's paintings was impressive.

film/movie/video about someone or something
> I saw a film about the Anasazi.
> The movie about Malcolm X was riveting.

game of something
> Would you like to play a game of chess?
> He invented the game of Scrabble.

play about someone or something
> The play about life in the ghetto was held over.
> They attended the play about John F. Kennedy.

postponement of something
> The postponement of the event was announced yesterday.
> Were the fans upset about the postponement of the game?

show about someone or something
> A show about sharks is on television this week.
> I watched a show about Albert Einstein.

song of something
> Their songs of love were very lyrical.
> Who writes songs of political protest?

Exercise 1

Fill in the blanks below with the correct noun.

Example: I have several <u>videos</u> about the Beatles.

1. He is giving a _____ of early romantic music.

2. The _____ of the fair disappointed the children.

3. We were sad about the _____ of our vacation plans; we had to wait another month.

4. He collects _____ about grammar.

5. The _____ about planets was very interesting.

show

books

concert

cancellation

postponement

Exercise 2

Circle the preposition that correctly completes the sentence.

Example: There is an exhibit _____ his work in Dean Hall.

     on   for   (of)

1. Let's play a game _____ backgammon.

     for   of   about

2. The play _____ Thomas Jefferson opens next week.

     from   in   about

3. We have tickets to a concert _____ early jazz.

     over   with   of

4. Who wrote "Song _____ the South"?

     for   in   of

Exercise 3

Read the first sentence; then complete the second sentence with a noun +
preposition.

Example: Will they cancel the lecture?
I read about the <u>cancellation of</u> the lecture.

1. The author postponed the reading.

    The _____ the reading surprised us.

2. The gallery owners are exhibiting their oil paintings.

    There is an _____ oil paintings at Gallery One.

3. She sang of her hometown.

    I knew all the _____ her hometown.

4. Who canceled the game?

    We had to change our plans because of the _____ the game.

5. The museum curator exhibited ancient vases.

    We enjoyed the _____ ancient vases.

Exercise 4

Circle the phrase that correctly completes the sentence.

1. I recorded a concert

    of chamber music.   about chamber music.

2. We played a game

    of cards.   about cards.

3. He bought me a book

    of national parks.   about national parks.

4. The children were entertained by a show

    of dinosaurs.   about dinosaurs.

Exercise 5

Read the first sentence; then complete the second sentence with a preposition + gerund noun phrase. Use the verb in the first sentence to make a gerund for the second sentence.

Example: They lived on a desert island.
We went to a play <u>about living on a desert island</u>.

1. She flies helicopters.

    She wrote a book _____.

2. They survived a hurricane.

    They watched a show _____.

3. He grew up in a small town.

    He made a movie _____.

4. The main character was a single mother.

    I went to a play _____.

5. He built ships.

    He watched a video _____.

6. We worked in a factory.

    We went to a movie _____.

Exercise 6

Complete these questions with the correct preposition.

Example: What was the film <u>about</u>?

1. What was the movie _____?

2. Who was the play _____?

3. What was the show _____?

4. What is there an exhibit _____?

5. Who is the book _____?

Exercise 7

Below is a list of events from the entertainment section of the local newspaper. Answer questions about the list in full sentences.

Example: What could you do on Sunday?
<u>On Sunday, I could bring a book about a favorite topic to the</u>
<u>library.</u>

1. What could you do on Saturday at 4:00?

   _____

2. What kind of songs does Louie Lewis sing?

   _____

3. Where is the play about Henry IV?

   _____

4. When does the movie about ghosts start?

   _____

Friday

7:00	Concert of early American music at the Heritage Museum
8:00	City Theater: *The Life of Henry IV*
9:00	Parthenon Bar: Louie Lewis featuring his new album *Love and Despair*

Saturday

12:00-4:00	Exhibit of Native American rugs: Lakota Gallery
4:00	Chess Tournament at Memorial Park
8:00	Jewel Cinema: *Ghosts Invade*

Sunday

| 2:00 | Bookathon: Bring books about favorite topics to the Peal Library. |

Unit B3: Language Learning

error in something

    Errors in pronunciation were always corrected.

    Did you make any errors in punctuation?

fluency in something

    Her fluency in Russian is amazing.

    Fluency in another language is an asset.

knowledge of something

    His knowledge of Spanish culture was immense.

    We were impressed by her knowledge of English grammar.

practice with something

    I need more practice with verb conjugation.

    The students asked for more practice with sentence formation.

proficiency in something

    Your proficiency in Japanese is impressive.

    He has little proficiency in Tagalog.

pronunciation of something

    The pronunciation of English vowels is difficult.

    My pronunciation of French is incomprehensible.

rule for something

    Do you know the rule for subject-verb agreement?

    We learned the rules for pronunciation.

translation from something into something else

    His translation from German into English was correct.

    Is translation from Mandarin into English difficult?

translation of something

    He is working on a translation of Arabic poetry.

    Her translation of Italian folksongs was welcomed.

understanding of something

    Their understanding of English grammar is quite good.

    My understanding of Portuguese is minimal.

Exercise 1

Fill in the blanks below with the correct noun.

Example: How is her proficiency in English?

1. The _____ of the *th* sound was easy for him.

2. For homework, she recommended _____ with idioms.

3. Did she make any _____ in pronunciation?

4. We are striving for _____ in English.

5. The _____ from English into Hebrew was difficult.

translation

errors

fluency

pronunciation

practice

Exercise 2

Circle the preposition that correctly completes the sentence.

Example: You can find the rule _____ contractions on page 43.

     on   in   (for)

1. Their proficiency _____ English was surprising.

     over   in   of

2. Success depended on their understanding _____ English grammar.

     on   in   of

3. She had a large vocabulary because of her knowledge _____ word formation.

     about   in   of

4. Practice _____ verbs was something everyone needed.

     with   in   of

Exercise 3

Read the first sentence; then complete the second sentence with a noun + preposition. Hint: If the verb or adjective is followed by a preposition, use that preposition. If the verb (other than *be*) is not followed by a preposition, use *of*.

Example: He erred in pronunciation.
He made an <u>error in</u> pronunciation.

1. We are proficient in three languages.

   We have _____ three languages.

2. They understood regional dialects.

   We were impressed by their _____ regional dialects.

3. She pronounced the word correctly.

   Her _____ the word was correct.

4. He knows the language well.

   He has a good _____ the language.

5. Are they fluent in a foreign language?

   Do they have _____ a foreign language?

6. I will translate the riddles.

   I will make a _____ the riddles.

Exercise 4

Read the first sentence; then complete the second sentence with an idiomatic noun phrase.

Example: The teacher pronounced each word carefully.
                  We appreciated the teacher's careful <u>pronunciation of each word</u>.

1. I want to be proficient in English.

   I want to achieve _____.

2. Do you know the language?

   Do you have any _____?

3. She erred in the translation.

   She made an _____.

4. They understand the story.

   Their _____ is astonishing.

5. The little girl is fluent in Greek.

   The little girl's _____ pleased her grandparents.

6. The student translated the joke.

   The student made a good _____.

Exercise 5

Complete these questions with the correct preposition.

Example: How many languages do you have proficiency <u>in</u>?

1. What do you need practice _____?

2. What did the student make an error _____?

3. What was the translation _____?

4. What languages do you have fluency _____?

5. Which verb do you need the rule _____?

Exercise 6

At the end of each language course, Mr. Rupert writes notes to his students. In these notes, he praises the students for their improvement and advises them of areas they need to work on. Read Mr. Rupert's comment to Natalie. Answer the questions about the note in full sentences.

Example: Why is Mr. Rupert congratulating Natalie?
<u>Mr. Rupert is congratulating Natalie because</u>
<u>her proficiency in English has improved.</u>

1. What is commendable?

   _____

2. What will Mr. Rupert always remember?

   _____

3. What does Natalie need more practice with?

   _____

4. What does Mr. Rupert think will improve?

   _____

Natalie,

Congratulations on your improved proficiency in English. Your knowledge of the language and your understanding of the culture are commendable. I will always remember your eloquent translation of Rilke's poetry. I hope you will continue your study of English. You might consider taking a conversation course. If you get more practice with spoken English, your fluency in English will continue to improve.

Best,
Mr. Rupert

Unit B4: Employment

application for something
   He sent his application for the job.
   Her application for the position was rejected.

characteristic of someone or something
   Motivation is a characteristic of a good worker.
   He described the characteristics of the job.

(in)competence in something
   She received a raise for her competence in marketing.
   He had to be retrained because of his incompetence in programming.

connection with someone
   He got the job because of his connection with the manager's family.
   She has a connection with someone in that firm.

consideration of something
   Thank you for your consideration of my application.
   I appreciate your consideration of my proposal.

contract for something
   I signed a contract for the job.
   The lawyer wrote a contract for the new position.

employment of someone
   Employment of minorities is one of the firm's leading priorities.
   The employment of female police officers was at an all-time low.

layoff of someone
   The layoff of the workers was not expected.
   He was angry about the layoff of his coworkers.

notification of something
   Notification of his dismissal came by mail.
   Notification of acceptance will be by phone.

strike against someone or something
   The mail carriers held a strike against the U.S. Postal Service.
   Who organized the strike against ABC Industry?

Exercise 1

Fill in the blanks below with the correct noun.

Example: The <u>layoff</u> of thirty employees was announced yesterday.

1. They mailed their _____ for
   a license.

2. His _____ for the position
   came in the mail today.

3. The _____ of three more
   workers is expected.

4. We need a _____ with
   someone in the auditor's office so we can get our
   permit.

5. After _____ of our financial
   status, we must withdraw our offer.

consideration

connection

layoff

application

contract

Exercise 2

Circle the preposition that correctly completes the sentence.

Example: When did you receive notification _____ the opening?

   on   with   (of)

1. My application _____ the job is being reviewed.

       for   in   with

2. Her competence _____ design was admired.

       with   in   for

3. Carelessness is not a characteristic _____ anyone who works here.

       over   for   of

4. The strike _____ the airlines lasted a month.

       of   in   against

Exercise 3

Read the first sentence; then complete the second sentence with a noun + preposition. Hint: If the verb or adjective is followed by a preposition, use that preposition. If the verb (other than *be*) is not followed by a preposition, use *of.*

Example: The company laid off twenty employees.
              There was a <u>layoff of</u> twenty employees.

1. You should consider the contract terms.

    We request your careful _____ the contract terms.

2. Did they notify you of your acceptance?

    Did you receive _____ your acceptance?

3. You applied for a job permit.

    You sent an _____ a job permit.

4. That behavior is characteristic of a good problem-solver.

    Perseverance is a _____ a good problem-solver.

5. He is competent in sales.

    His _____ sales earned him a bonus.

6. Will they strike against us?

    Will they hold a _____ us?

Exercise 4

Read the first sentence; then complete the second sentence with an idiomatic noun phrase.

Example: The company laid off fifteen employees.
          The newspaper reported a <u>layoff of fifteen employees</u>.

1. They contracted for the job.

   They signed a _____.

2. We are employing three new secretaries.

   We expect the _____.

3. I wasn't connected with anybody.

   I had no _____.

4. Are they considering your proposal?

   How long will their _____ take?

5. They notified us of the pay raise.

   The _____ came yesterday.

6. Many people applied for the job.

   We received more than three hundred _____.

Exercise 5

Complete these questions with the correct preposition.

Example: Which position was the application <u>for</u>?

1. Who did you have a connection _____?

2. What type of work was the contract _____?

3. What field is he incompetent _____?

4. What did they receive notification _____?

5. Which company was the strike _____?

Exercise 6

XYZ Industries mailed a letter inviting people to apply for jobs at their new factory. Answer the questions about this letter in full sentences.

Example: What is XYZ Industries inviting?
<u>XYZ Industries is inviting applications for jobs at their new factory.</u>

1. What is XYZ Industries anticipating?

    _____

2. How long will the consideration of applications last?

    _____

3. What are the characteristics of a good applicant?

    _____

XYZ Industries
Dollar Way
Plaintown, Iowa 87342

Dear Sir or Madam:

We would like to invite you to apply for a job at our new factory. We anticipate the employment of thirty workers. A list of openings is enclosed with this letter. We will be considering applications for the next two months. If you have enthusiasm and drive, we encourage you to apply.

Sincerely,

XYZ Industries

Unit B5: Harm and Safety

awareness of something

> There is little awareness of the dangers of alcohol.
> We need increased awareness of boating safety procedures.

chance of something

> The chance of accidental death is great.
> There is no chance of an earthquake here.

danger of something

> The public does not comprehend the danger of floods.
> Is there any danger of wildfires along the river?

defense against someone or something

> Is there any defense against predators?
> The best defense against a natural disaster is preparation.

destruction of something

> The destruction of the city was terrifying.
> The destruction of the factory saddened everyone.

freedom from something

> We sought freedom from harm.
> They fought for freedom from their rulers.

neglect of something

> Neglect of proper maintenance might result in an accident.
> His neglect of the house made it dangerous to live in.

protection from something

> Our school needs protection from gangs.
> The new structures provide protection from earthquakes.

safety from someone or something

> The police provide safety from crime.
> We discussed safety from surprise attacks.

security against someone or something

> Dogs provide security against intruders.
> He mentioned security against theft as a primary goal.

Exercise 1

Fill in the blanks below with the correct noun.

Example: He asked for <u>protection</u> from a bully.

1. Don't worry, there is no _____ of famine in the area.

2. They search for _____ from gang activity.

3. The _____ of unsafe driving practices comes through education.

4. The _____ of private property is illegal.

5. Their _____ against flood damage included sandbags.

defense
awareness
destruction
danger
freedom

Exercise 2

Circle the preposition that correctly completes the sentence.

Example: Students need more than awareness _____ first aid.

on   for   (of)

1. The coach made safety _____ injury a priority.

for   from   with

2. The vault provides security _____ theft.

against   in   for

3. What is the chance _____ victory?

over   with   of

4. Police wanted to lessen the danger _____ a riot.

for   in   of

Exercise 3

Read the first sentence; then complete the second sentence with a noun + preposition. Hint: If the verb or adjective is followed by a preposition, use that preposition. If the verb (other than *be*) is not followed by a preposition, use *of*.

Example: They want to be freed from oppression.
They want <u>freedom from</u> oppression.

1. A bomb destroyed the building.

    The _____ the building was due to a bomb.

2. Preventative medicine defends against disease.

    Preventative medicine is the best _____ disease.

3. The children were aware of safety procedures.

    The children's _____ safety procedures was remarkable.

4. He neglects his civic responsibilities.

    His _____ civic responsibilities made others angry.

5. We were protected from the angry crowd.

    We sought _____ the angry crowd.

6. Is anyone safe from the secret police?

    Did anyone find _____ the secret police?

Exercise 4

Read the first sentence; then complete the second sentence with an idiomatic noun phrase.

Example: They were secure against attack.
                    They sought <u>security against attack.</u>

1. Are we safe from harm?

   We prayed for _____.

2. They were not protected from the authorities.

   They wanted _____.

3. They neglect their parental duties.

   We noted their _____.

4. We were aware of the war.

   There was _____.

5. He defended himself against attack.

   His _____ was successful.

6. The forest was destroyed.

   A carelessly thrown cigarette caused the _____.

Exercise 5

Change these sentences into questions. The *wh-* word replaces the underlined word(s).

Example: Car alarms provide security against <u>car theft</u>.
What <u>do car alarms provide security against?</u>

1. We have freedom from <u>illegal searches</u>.

   What _____?

2. They increased awareness of <u>gang activity</u>.

   What _____?

3. Vitamin C is a defense against <u>colds</u>.

   What _____?

Exercise 6

Answer the questions, using the list of things that will keep you safe from harm.

Example: What has decreased the danger of accidental poisoning?
<u>Child-proof medicine containers have decreased the danger of accidental poisoning.</u>

1. What do we use for protection from the sun's harmful rays?

   _____

2. What do we use for safety from fires?

   _____

3. What provides defense against bike thieves?

   _____

4. What can lessen the danger of drowning?

   _____

sunscreen
child-proof
medicine containers
bike locks
burglar alarms
fire alarms
flotation devices
seat belts
safety deposit boxes

Unit B6: Friends and Enemies

acceptance of someone
> Their acceptance of him into their club was unanticipated.
> I yearned for the acceptance of my family.

(dis)agreement with someone
> He has an agreement with his neighbors.
> What caused her disagreement with us?

aggression toward someone
> That nation's aggression toward its neighbor was unexpected.
> I don't understand her aggression toward all newcomers.

alliance with/against someone or something
> We formed an alliance with them.
> They formed an alliance against us.

appreciation of someone or something
> We showed our appreciation of him and his work.
> She mentioned her appreciation of my companionship.

association with someone or something
> Our association with him has lasted a long time.
> His association with the team spanned two decades.

betrayal of someone or something
> Her betrayal of our friendship was not surprising.
> My betrayal of the club was unforgivable.

confidence in someone or something
> We have confidence in his ability to succeed.
> I lost confidence in my old friend.

contact with someone
> I haven't stayed in contact with my childhood friends.
> Contact with friends is sometimes hard to maintain.

triumph/victory over someone or something
> They exulted in their triumph over us.
> Victory over the small nation was assured.

Exercise 1

Fill in the blanks below with the correct noun.

Example: They prayed for <u>victory</u> over their enemies.

1. He has not been in _____ with his former wife.

2. Her _____ with her classmate resulted in an argument.

3. We have total _____ in them.

4. Nations form _____ with other nations for protection.

5. We hated him for his _____ of our secret.

alliances

confidence

contact

betrayal

disagreement

Exercise 2

Circle the preposition that correctly completes the sentence.

Example: Their disagreement _____ the powerful nation resulted in war.

     (with)   in   against

1. Our alliance _____ them instituted a boycott.

     of   in   against

2. We wanted victory _____ war and disease.

     on   in   over

3. How can I show my appreciation _____ her effort?

     about   on   of

4. She was convicted of betrayal _____ her nation.

     on   in   of

Exercise 3a

Read the first sentence; then complete the second sentence with a noun + preposition.

Example: Italy allied itself with Germany.
We were afraid of Italy's <u>alliance with</u> Germany.

1. Do you appreciate his help?

   Have you expressed your _____ his help?

2. He betrayed their cause.

   His _____ their cause earned him their contempt.

3. The country was extremely aggressive toward its eastern neighbor.

   The country's _____ its eastern neighbor was sudden and harsh.

4. You triumphed over your opponent.

   Your _____ your opponent surprised everyone.

5. Surprisingly, they allied themselves with us.

   Surprisingly, they formed an _____ us.

6. They associate with very important people in the government.

   Their _____ these people helps their careers.

Exercise 3b

To confide in someone and *to have confidence in someone* have different meanings. Fill in the blank with the correct form.

1. I _____ you because I know you won't tell anyone else what I say.

2. I _____ you. I know you'll make a good director.

Exercise 4a

Read the first sentence; then complete the second sentence with an idiomatic noun phrase.

Example: We agreed with them.
Our <u>agreement with them</u> was marked by a handshake.

1. He has been associated with the club since 1980.

    His _____ began in 1980.

2. I totally agree with you.

    I'm in total _____.

3. They have allied against us.

    How should we respond to their _____?

4. They appreciated our friendship.

    Their _____ never went unnoticed

5. You betrayed your country.

    Your _____ will not be forgiven.

6. Paulus triumphed over everyone.

    We hailed Paulus's _____.

Exercise 4b

How is the relation between the two sentences below different from that in the sentences above?

I didn't contact you.

I didn't stay in contact with you.

Exercise 5

Change these sentences into questions. The *wh-* word replaces the underlined word(s). Remember to change first-person pronouns to second-person pronouns

Example: My agreement was with <u>the vice president of the company</u>.
            Who <u>was your agreement with?</u>

1. She had a disagreement with her teacher about <u>the answer</u>.

    What _____?

2. They had an alliance with <u>the king</u>.

    Who _____?

3. <u>His boss</u> had great confidence in him.

    Who _____?

4. I have been in contact with <u>many of my classmates</u>.

    Who _____?

5. <u>Juan</u> led his team to victory over France.

    Who _____?

Exercise 6

Read the letter below. Answer the questions about this letter in full sentences.

Example: Did Lilly mention her appreciation of the flowers Sandra brought?

<u>Yes, Lilly mentioned her appreciation of the flowers Sandra brought.</u>

1. Who was in agreement with Lilly?

   _____

2. What did Lilly tell everyone about?

   _____

3. Lilly apologized for the possible betrayal of something. What was it?

   _____

4. Who should Sandra be in contact with if she wants theater tickets?

   _____

Dear Sandra,
Thank you for helping me with the party. I especially appreciated the flowers. Everyone agreed with me when I said they were the most beautiful roses in the city. I also wanted to apologize for telling everyone you accepted a new job. Later I thought that perhaps you didn't want everyone to know just yet. I hope I didn't betray a secret.
Your friend,
Lilly

P.S. If you want tickets to the play, contact Stefan.

Unit B7: Education

analysis of something
> His analysis of the substance was accurate.
> We had to write an analysis of the play.

course in something
> I took three courses in geography this quarter.
> I have to take a course in computer science this spring.

education of someone
> The education of our children is important.
> The parents were concerned about the education of their son.

exam/examination/quiz/test on something or in a subject
> We have a quiz on that chapter tomorrow.
> Today the teacher is giving an exam in physics.

instruction in something
> He went to a community college for instruction in technical writing.
> Instruction in foreign languages is offered at the public library.

interest in something
> Their interest in traditional music is inspiring.
> Do they have any interest in the subject?

major in something
> He has a major in English.
> The student decided on a major in anthropology.

paper on something
> We wrote a paper on desert wildlife.
> His paper on changing weather patterns was well documented.

research on something
> Her research on earthquakes will help us predict them.
> He did his research on Native American tribes of the Southwest.

study of something
> Their study of viruses will be published next month.
> For my final project, I'll report on my study of child prodigies.

Exercise 1

Fill in the blanks below with the correct noun.

Example: He began his <u>research</u> on the topic a year ago.

1. She wrote a _____ on Latin American art.

2. We are having an _____ in math.

3. Their _____ of ancient tools was remarkable.

4. He received _____ in computer programming.

5. Her _____ of the infant's behavior was thorough.

instruction

study

paper

analysis

exam

Exercise 2

Circle the preposition that correctly completes the sentence.

Example: The government paid for the education _____ the refugees.

      on   in   (of)

1. The analysis _____ the problem is due on Monday.

      over   in   of

2. She graduated with a major _____ mathematics.

      on   in   about

3. Over the weekend, I wrote a paper _____ folktales.

      on   in   of

4. His study _____ local canyons was fascinating.

      for   in   of

Exercise 3

Read the first sentence; then complete the second sentence with a noun + preposition.

Example: He studied frogs.
His <u>study of</u> frogs lasted four years.

1. I analyzed the problem.

   The _____ the problem was difficult.

2. He majored in psychology.

   He has a _____ psychology.

3. She studies rats.

   Her _____ rats won an award.

4. The grandparents educated the child.

   The grandparents paid for the _____ the child.

5. They instructed him in the use of the machine.

   He received _____ the use of the machine.

6. The instructor tested us on three chapters.

   At the end of the month, we had a _____ three chapters.

Exercise 4a

Read the first sentence; then complete the second sentence with an idiomatic noun phrase.

Example: The teacher instructed us in music theory.
Our <u>instruction in music theory</u> was very good.

1. The program educated teenagers about the harmful effects of drugs.

   They hoped the _____ would discourage drug use.

2. The instructor tested us in social studies.

   The _____ was easy.

3. He majored in geology this year.

   He has a _____.

4. They studied ancient paintings.

   Their _____ was funded by the museum.

5. She analyzed the sentence.

   Her _____ was correct.

6. Will you quiz me on chapter 1?

   Will you give me a _____?

Exercise 4b

What do you notice about the following sentences?

The professor instructed the students in Eastern religions.

The instruction of the students was challenging.

The instruction in Eastern religions was thorough.

▌Exercise 5

Change these sentences into questions. The *wh-* word replaces the underlined word(s). Remember to change first-person pronouns to second-person pronouns.

Example: I will have to take my final exam in psychology <u>on Monday</u>.
              When <u>do you have to take your final exam in psychology</u>?

1. She has a major in <u>biology</u>.

   What _____?

2. His research was on <u>child development</u>.

   What _____?

3. I wrote a paper on <u>the French Revolution</u>.

   What _____?

4. They are taking courses in <u>astronomy and political science</u> this semester.

   What _____ this semester?

5. <u>We</u> did a study of Gothic architecture.

   Who _____?

Exercise 6

Look at Julia's schedule for next week. Answer the questions about her schedule in full sentences.

---

exam wetland conservation — Monday
paper women poets — Tuesday
quiz algebra — Wednesday
study due — Thursday
psychology research presentation — Friday

Example: When does Julia take an exam on wetland conservation?
            Julia takes an exam on wetland conservation on Monday.

1. When is Julia's study of motivation due?

    _____

2. When is her paper on women poets due?

    _____

3. When does Julia take a quiz on algebraic equations?

    _____

4. When does she present her research on motivation?

    _____

bill for something or some amount

I received a bill for the furniture.
He got a bill for $10.

charge of some amount

There was an extra charge of $5 for the delivery.
A charge of only $3 is fair.

check for something or some amount

He sent a check for the delivery.
I wrote a check for $10.

cost of something

What was the cost of the new machine?
The cost of the new building was very high.

credit of some amount

I asked for a credit of $20.
He was given a credit of $30.

distribution of something

Distribution of the new product will begin tomorrow.
The distribution of work was fair.

order for something

The order for the new computers was delayed.
Your order for new phones arrived today.

price of something

The price of paper has risen.
What is the price of the stock?

production of something

Production of the new software was delayed.
The production of a new system takes time.

tax on something

Some states have no tax on clothing.
They resented the tax on gasoline.

Exercise 1

Fill in the blanks below with the correct noun.

Example: The <u>cost</u> of electricity is high.

1. Is there a _____ on cigarettes?

2. The _____ of success is hard work.

3. Your _____ for pencils will be filled immediately.

4. When does _____ of the new software begin?

5. Who paid the _____ for the delivery?

> production
>
> tax
>
> bill
>
> order
>
> price

Exercise 2

Circle the preposition that correctly completes the sentence.

Example: A credit _____ $100 was issued to your account.

     on   with   (of)

1. The bill _____ the service was too high.

     for   in   with

2. What is the price _____ the item?

     with   of   for

3. He gave me a check _____ $75.

     over   for   of

4. We asked about the tax _____ the materials.

     of   in   on

Exercise 3a

Read the first sentence; then complete the second sentence with a noun +
preposition.

Example: The new machine cost a lot.
              The <u>cost of</u> the new machine was high.

1. We produce computer parts.

    The _____ computer parts is time-consuming.

2. They distribute computer parts.

    The _____ computer parts begins in six weeks.

3. They charged us $60.

    Their _____ $60 was for extra work.

4. He credited us $60.

    A _____ $60 was issued to our account.

5. How much does new lighting cost?

    What is the _____ new lighting?

Exercise 3b

Which preposition did you use in each of the sentences above? _____

Exercise 3c

Read the following sentences.

The government taxes alcohol.
The tax on alcohol is high.

We ordered six chairs.
The order for six chairs was delayed.

How are the above pairs different from the sentences in 3a?

Exercise 4

Read the first sentence; then complete the second sentence with an idiomatic noun phrase.

Example: They billed him for the new computers.
He paid the <u>bill for the new computers</u>.

1. Could you credit my account for $70?

    I asked for a _____.

2. They charged us $100.

    We think a _____ is too high.

3. Overtime is distributed according to seniority.

    He complained about the _____.

4. He ordered new desks.

    He received the _____ yesterday.

5. The product is priced too high.

    The _____ is too high.

6. That state taxes everything.

    That state has a _____.

Exercise 5

Change these sentences into questions. The *wh-* word replaces the underlined word(s).

Example: The check was for $20.
How much <u>was the check for?</u>

1. The check was for <u>a new dress</u>.

   What _____?

2. I paid a bill for <u>$375</u>.

   How much _____?

3. The bill was for <u>the car insurance</u>.

   What _____?

4. They charged tax on <u>his lunch</u>.

   What _____?

Bernie Garcia is opening a new business. He will sell office equipment. The following are a few of his start-up costs. Answer the questions about this information in full sentences.

	COST	TAX
Building	$75,000	$5775
Lights	$1,000	$77
Furniture	$2,000	$154
Carpet	$800	$61
Cleaning service	$250	$19

Example: What did he pay a charge of $250 for?
<u>He paid a charge of $250 for the cleaning service.</u>

1. What was the cost of the building?

_____

2. What was the price of the carpet?

_____

3. What was the tax on the carpet?

_____

4. How much was the bill for the furniture (including tax)?

_____

5. What was the price of the lights?

_____

Unit B9: Health

cure for something

    The cure for cancer has not been found yet.

    Researchers are looking for a cure for AIDS.

diagnosis of something

    The diagnosis of the disease is the first step toward a cure.

    The diagnosis of the disease was made by several doctors.

growth in something

    The baby's growth in height and weight was normal.

    There was no growth in the number of stroke patients this year.

head of something

    The head of the pediatrics department gave a lecture.

    The head of the department attended the patient.

improvement in something

    We noticed much improvement in his health.

    They were pleased with the improvement in her walking.

injection of something

    They gave him an injection of something to relieve the pain.

    An injection of the drug put him to sleep.

prescription for something

    The doctors gave him a prescription for a pain reliever.

    The pharmacist filled the prescription for a sleeping aid.

prognosis for something

    The prognosis for my disease was hopeful.

    We were happy with his prognosis for the illness.

treatment for something

    Treatment for cancer often includes chemotherapy.

    The treatment for my illness was routine.

vaccination against something

    I was given a vaccination against measles.

    Vaccinations against the flu will be given on Thursday.

Exercise 1

Fill in the blanks below with the correct noun.

Example: Who is the <u>head</u> of the department?

1. He noticed a _____ in the size of the patient's tumor.

2. Has there been any _____ in her condition?

3. The _____ of the illness was wrong.

4. She used a needle to give me an _____ of Novocain.

5. The doctor called in a _____ for pain medication.

prescription

injection

improvement

growth

diagnosis

Exercise 2

Circle the preposition that correctly completes the sentence.

Example: Treatment _____ the disease requires a hospital stay.

    on   (for)   in

1. We all were given vaccinations _____ diphtheria.

    on   in   against

2. She hopes there will be a cure _____ migraine headaches.

    with   in   for

3. Dr. Gaskill is the head _____ the hematology department.

    over   for   of

4. They issued a prognosis _____ her recovery.

    for   in   with

Exercise 3

Read the first sentence; then complete the second sentence with a noun +
preposition.

Example: The doctors cured the girl's disease.
              There was a <u>cure for</u> her disease.

1. My mother was treated for diabetes.

   My mother received _____ diabetes.

2. Were you vaccinated against the measles?

   Did you receive a _____ the measles?

3. The doctor prescribed flurazepam.

   He received a _____ flurazepam.

4. She diagnosed the condition as gout.

   The doctor reported her _____ gout.

5. The nurse injected her with insulin.

   She received an _____ insulin.

6. I wish I could cure my cold.

   I wish I could find a _____ my cold.

Exercise 4

Read the first sentence; then complete the second sentence with an idiomatic noun phrase.

Example: The patient improved in his speech.
The patient showed much <u>improvement in his speech</u>.

1. He will cure your illness.

   He thinks there is a _____.

2. The doctor prescribed an ointment.

   The doctor wrote a _____.

3. The number of kidney donors has grown.

   The paper reported a _____.

4. My daughter was vaccinated against polio.

   My daughter received a _____.

5. The dentist will inject Novocain.

   The dentist will give you an _____.

6. I can treat your condition.

   The _____ is expensive.

Exercise 5

Change these sentences into questions. The *wh-* word replaces the underlined word(s). Remember to change first-person pronouns to second-person pronouns.

Example: She found cures for <u>several diseases</u>.
What <u>did she find cures for</u>?

1. The best treatment for the flu is <u>bed rest</u>.

   What _____?

2. <u>Jane</u> never received a vaccination against the measles.

   Who _____?

3. She is the head of <u>cardiology</u>.

   What department _____?

4. There has been a growth in <u>the number of heart patients</u> this year.

   What _____ this year?

5. Mary's prescription for eye drops will be delivered <u>tomorrow</u>.

   When _____?

Exercise 6

Your friend's mother calls from Egypt, asking about the health of her son, Omar. Using your notes, answer her questions.

Example: Did he see the head of the dermatology department?
<u>Yes, he saw the head of the dermatology department.</u>

1. Did he receive a prescription for something?

   _____

2. Is the prognosis for recovery good?

   _____

3. How soon will he see improvement in his condition?

   _____

- Dr. Silvis, head of dermatology
- Has improved
- Prescription — Dermalotion
- Should be well in 3–4 days

Unit Bio: Science and Technology

argument against/for something
> Their argument for the new plant was weak.
> There is no argument against our position.

competition for something
> Is there any competition for the new lab job?
> The competition for the prize was stiff.

connection between some things
> They proved a connection between cholesterol and heart disease.
> Is there any connection between the two facts?

deviation from something
> They studied all deviations from the norm.
> My score was a deviation from previous scores.

difference between some things
> There is no difference between his account and yours.
> What is the difference between a solid and a liquid?

evidence against/for something
> There was no evidence for his conclusion.
> The evidence against his testimony was overwhelming.

expert in something
> He is an expert in physics.
> She is an expert in her field.

inferiority/superiority in something
> Inferiority in marketing resulted in lost revenue.
> Their goal was superiority in design.

monopoly on something
> Does the company have a monopoly on word processors?
> They maintain a monopoly on oil production.

rationale for something
> They stated the rationale for their experiment.
> The rationale for the investigation included public benefit.

Exercise 1

Fill in the blanks below with the correct noun.

Example: They were involved in a <u>competition</u> for best design.

1. His _____ against the new construction was unconvincing.

2. Who provided the _____ for expansion?

3. The _____ in chemical engineering will give a lecture today.

4. Some _____ from the first measurement was expected.

5. There was a huge _____ between the two conclusions.

difference

deviation

argument

expert

rationale

Exercise 2

Circle the preposition that correctly completes the sentence.

Example: Is there any difference _____ capitalism and competition?

    with   in   (between)

1. Their superiority _____ production is astounding.

    of   in   against

2. The empirical evidence _____ the theory was impressive.

    on   for   over

3. Did you enter the competition _____ funding?

    about   on   for

4. My boss has a monopoly _____ my time.

    on   in   of

Exercise 3

Read the first sentence; then complete the second sentence with a noun + preposition. Hint: If the verb or adjective is followed by a preposition, use that preposition. If the verb refers to a relation between two things, use *between*.

Example: They argued against the procedure.
             Their <u>argument against</u> the procedure is plausible.

1. Did your answer deviate from the expected results?

   Was there any _____ the expected results?

2. They competed for consumer dollars.

   They are leading the _____ consumer dollars.

3. Factory life and private life were closely connected during this period.

   The _____ factory life and private life was close.

4. The two computers differ very little.

   The _____ the two computers is minimal.

5. Our experiment was judged superior in design.

   We were praised for our _____ experimental design.

6. We must argue for a different strategy.

   We must make an _____ a different strategy.

Exercise 4

Read the first sentence; then complete the second sentence with a preposition + gerund noun phrase. Use the verb in the first sentence to make a gerund for the second sentence.

Example: We believe him.
There is no evidence <u>for believing him</u>.

1. They should support the investigation.

   Their rationale _____ was printed in the newspaper.

2. Kim designs software.

   He is an expert _____.

3. There is no reason they shouldn't build a new factory.

   Is there any argument _____?

4. Many companies create user-friendly software.

   There is competition _____.

5. People who eat fatty foods often suffer from heart disease.

   There is a proven connection _____.

6. Only Amax manufactures that product.

   Amax has a monopoly _____.

▌Exercise 5

Supply the correct preposition. Then change the sentence into a yes/no question.

Example: He gave a rationale <u>for</u> continuing the work.
<u>Did he give a rationale for continuing the work?</u>

1. He had a good argument _____ investing.

_____?

2. She is an expert _____ amphibian anatomy.

_____?

3. There is fierce competition _____ the $10,000 prize.

_____?

4. They found a connection _____ the robbery and someone in her office.

_____?

5. That company has a monopoly _____ baseball bats.

_____?

Exercise 6

Read the news report below. Answer the questions about this report in full sentences.

Example: What did experts from Mid-Cosmos Corporation report?
<u>Experts from Mid-Cosmos Corporation reported evidence for life on Mars.</u>

1. Who reported evidence for life on Mars?

    _____

2. What did their argument include?

    _____

3. What has the corporation been accused of?

    _____

4. What are the employees of Mid-Cosmos Corporation experts in?

    _____

Today experts in space travel from Mid-Cosmos Corporation reported evidence for life on Mars. Their argument for travel to that planet included rationale for government subsidies. It should be noted that Mid-Cosmos Corporation has been accused of having a monopoly on space-travel vehicles.

Unit B11: Economy

(dis)advantage of something
> What is the advantage of this new policy?
> The disadvantages of the proposal outweigh its advantages.

cause of something
> The cause of their discontent is high taxes.
> Slow growth is the cause of unemployment.

cut/hike in something
> There will be a hike in taxes this year.
> What do you think about the cut in welfare benefits?

damage to someone or something
> The damage to our present standard of living will be severe.
> How will we recover from this damage to our economy?

decrease/increase in something
> Will there be an increase in tax revenue this year?
> There was a decrease in defense spending this year.

demand for something
> There isn't a demand for record players.
> Has the demand for good service been met?

fall/rise in something
> A fall in unemployment is predicted.
> A rise in inflation is expected this year.

reason for something
> Did he give any reason for raising taxes?
> The reason for the new policy was that the economy had improved.

reduction in something
> A reduction in spending would help solve the budget deficit.
> There was a reduction in funding for education this year.

solution to something
> The politician said that the solution to our problems is a tax cut.
> Is there a solution to the budget deficit?

Exercise 1

Fill in the blanks below with the correct noun.

Example: He has proposed a <u>cut</u> in taxes.

1. No one expected a _____ in interest rates.

2. The _____ to the politician's credibility could not be undone.

3. The _____ of the economic upswing was not clear.

4. He predicts a sharp _____ in the value of the dollar.

5. Do you see the _____ of that country's economic policy?

cause

fall

rise

advantage

damage

Exercise 2

Circle the preposition that correctly completes the sentence.

Example: Will he propose a cut _____ small-business taxes?

(in)   for   of

1. The demand _____ simplified tax forms has grown.

    for   in   of

2. He promised there would be no hike _____ taxes this year.

    on   in   about

3. Has there been a reduction _____ the funding of the arts?

    about   in   of

4. A cut _____ social security may have adverse effects.

    on   in   of

Exercise 3

Read the first sentence; then complete the second sentence with a noun + preposition. Hint: If the verb in the first sentence refers to an increase or decrease, the related noun will often be followed by *in*.

Example: Prices rose.
There was a <u>rise in</u> prices.

1. We will solve the problem.

   The _____ the problem is being discussed.

2. That policy damaged the country's social structure.

   The _____ the country's social structure was extensive.

3. The public has demanded some kind of tax relief.

   There has been a great _____ some kind of tax relief.

4. Interest rates rose.

   The _____ interest rates angered new homeowners.

5. The number of people on welfare has decreased this month.

   There has been a _____ the number of people on welfare.

6. What caused the economic decline?

   What was the _____ the economic decline?

Exercise 4

Read the first sentence; then complete the second sentence with an idiomatic noun phrase.

Example: The legislature cut the gasoline tax.
The legislature proposed a <u>cut in the gasoline tax</u>.

1. No one knew what caused the recession.

   The _____ was unknown.

2. The new economic treaty damaged our relations with that country.

   The _____ may be irreversible.

3. The students demanded more funding for education.

   The students' _____ was ignored.

4. Will our economic problems be solved?

   Is there a _____?

5. The value of their currency fell slightly.

   There was a slight _____.

6. Employment opportunities have increased.

   Did you hear about the _____?

Exercise 5

Change these sentences into yes/no questions. Supply the correct prepositions.

Example: There was a reduction _____ the amount of paperwork.
<u>Was there a reduction in the amount of paperwork?</u>

1. The president is worrying about a fall _____ stock prices.

   _____?

2. There is high demand _____ employees with technical skills.

   _____?

3. The task force will propose a solution _____ the crisis.

   _____?

4. The failing economy is the cause _____ the tension between the government and the people.

   _____?

5. He recommended a cut _____ spending.

   _____?

Exercise 6

The following headlines appeared in your local newspaper. Use them to answer the questions below. Your answers should be full sentences that include noun + preposition combinations.

Example: What is the cause of discontent?
<u>A state tax hike is the cause of discontent.</u>

1. Has there been a rise in inflation?

   _____

2. Has a solution to the deficit been reported?

   _____

3. What has damage to the economy been attributed to?

   _____

4. Has there been a rise in the unemployment rate?

   _____

5. Who is promising a cut in taxes?

   _____

STATE TAX HIKE CAUSES DISCONTENT

INFLATION RISES 2%

PRESIDENT PROMISES FEDERAL TAX CUT

UNEMPLOYMENT RATE FALLS

INTERNATIONAL TRADE AGREEMENT DAMAGES ECONOMY

SEUBERT SOLVES DEFICIT

C

Prepositional Phrases

Units C1 through C8 cover prepositional phrases that are set idiomatic expressions (e.g., *in time* and *as a result*). Units C9 through C11 present multiword prepositional phrases, whose object form varies (e.g., *in front of someone or something*).

The prepositional phrases chosen for each unit all refer to a specific context (e.g., buying and selling) or concept (e.g., reference). Prepositional phrases that are related in some way are listed together.

Unit C₁: Time

at once: *immediately*
> Come here at once.
> You must go at once.

at times: *sometimes*
> At times, I feel very sad.
> That television show is very funny at times.

for a while: *for an unspecified period of time*
> We talked for a while.
> They stayed in Seattle for a while.

for once: *on one occasion (that something should occur more often is implied)*
> For once, he completed his assignment.
> The weather prediction was right for once.

in the meantime: *in the period of time between two events*
> She will be moving to Santa Fe in three months. In the meantime, she can stay with us.
> Mark starts his new job next month. In the meantime, he'll continue as manager here.

in this day and age: *in modern times*
> In this day and age, many people are vaccinated against smallpox.
> Many people are superstitious even in this day and age.

in time: *with enough time*
> Did you get there in time to hear the opening remarks?
> We met at the theater in time to have coffee before the play started.

on time: *punctual or in a punctual manner*
> He finished on time.
> Were you on time for the meeting?

out of date: *no longer fashionable or useful*
> That research is out of date.
> Medical knowledge becomes out of date quickly.

to date: *until and including the present point in time*
> To date, only three hundred people have signed the petition.
> This is his best film to date.

Exercise 1

Choose a word from the box to complete each prepositional phrase below.

Example: He found his coat and left at <u>once</u>.

1. There have been no cancellations to
   _____.

2. Mozart's symphonies will never be out of
   _____.

3. Let's study for a _____ and
   then go to the cafeteria.

4. Even the library can be noisy at
   _____.

5. Turn in your papers on
   _____.

age
date
day
meantime
once
time
times
while

6. We were in _____ for our plane.

7. You were right for _____.

8. Our books haven't arrived yet, so in the _____ we'll use
   photocopies.

9. Changes need to be made at _____.

10. In this _____ and _____, students can
    research almost anything on the Internet.

Exercise 2

Circle the preposition that correctly completes the sentence.

Example: The senators filed in and the meeting started _____ once.

      in   (at)   on

1. _____ times, it can be very windy here.

      In   At   On

2. Before discussing business, we chatted _____ a while.

      for   on   out of

3. The company's sick-leave policy is _____ date.

      in   on   out of

4. Employees should come to work _____ time.

      at   on   in

5. _____ this day and age, most people live longer than their parents did.

      In   On   For

6. _____ once, he did what he was told.

      For   On   In

7. They didn't arrive _____ time to see the parade.

      at   in   for

8. Our new assignment doesn't begin for a month, and we're finished with the current one, so what do we do _____ the meantime?

      at   on   in

▎Exercise 3

Rewrite the sentences, replacing the underlined part with an idiomatic prepositional phrase.

Example: At the present point in time, six people have announced that they are running for office.
To date, six people have announced that they are running for office.

1. The plane was punctual.

   _____

2. On one occasion, my dog actually came when I called her.

   _____

3. Toss the pasta with the oil and serve it immediately.

   _____

4. We arrived with enough time to find front-row seats.

   _____

5. This machine is no longer useful.

   _____

6. His plane wasn't scheduled to leave for three hours, so between 2:00 and 5:00, he played video games.

   _____

7. Sometimes my mom suffers from terrible headaches.

   _____

8. Let's think about this for some time before we make our decision.

   _____

Exercise 4

Below is the schedule for the opening of the new mall in town. You arrived at the mall at 10:00. It is now 11:00. Your friend Erin is supposed to meet you at 11:00, but you haven't seen her yet. Your friend Joe is going to arrive at 1:00. Read the schedule below; then answer the questions about it.

MID-TOWN MALL GRAND OPENING

10:00	Mayor Hanson's Welcome
	Free Midtown Mall Mugs
11:00	**Midtown High School Choir** Performance in the Atrium
12:00	Free Hot Dogs and Pop at the **Double Dog Stand**
1:00	**Martin's Bookstore** One-Hour Magazine Sale
2:00	Free Ice Cream Cones at the **Whippy Dip Ice Cream Shop**
3:00	**Jazz Band** Performance in the Atrium
4:00	Shop-Until-You-Drop Sale at All Clothing Stores
5:00	Free Coffee or Tea at the **Atrium Café**

Example: Who arrived in time to hear the mayor and receive a free mug?
<u>I arrived in time to hear the mayor and receive a free mug.</u>

1. Who isn't on time?

    _____

2. If Erin doesn't show up, and Joe isn't arriving until 1:00, what could you do in the meantime?

    _____

3. Who won't arrive in time to get a free hot dog?

    _____

4. If you want to hear the choir, where should you go at once?

    _____

5. You have to catch your bus at 3:15. What could you do for a while before you leave?

    _____

Unit C2: Sequence

at this point: *at this time or stage*
>We have nothing to say at this point.
>What should we do at this point?

for a start: *first*
>He would make a great leader. For a start, he would organize our efforts.
>The weather in the North is harsh. For a start, it can snow very early.

in addition: *additionally*
>The politician said he wouldn't raise taxes. In addition, he promised to make loans easier to get.
>I am fluent in Hebrew and Farsi. In addition, I can read Arabic, although I can't speak it.

in conclusion
>*This phrase signals a concluding point.*
>In conclusion, a new computer lab would benefit our university greatly.

in line: *waiting in traffic or in a row of people in order to take one's turn*
>We stood in line in front of the copier.
>How long did you wait in line?

in/out of order: *according or not according to sequence*
>That name is out of order. *Janet* comes after *Jane.*
>They did the workbook exercises in order.

in sum
>*This phrase introduces a summary.*
>In sum, both companies have agreed to the merger.

in the end
>*This phrase signals a conclusion arrived at after much consideration.*
>We spent months planning the fair, but in the end, we had to cancel it because we didn't have enough money.

in the first place: *before a series of events happened*
>What brought him to the United States in the first place?
>She said we should have consulted a specialist in the first place.

in the first/second place: *first/second*
>He couldn't have committed the crime. In the first place, he has an alibi.
>In the second place, there is no motive.

Exercise 1

Choose a word from the box to complete each prepositional phrase below.

Example: At this <u>point</u>, we should review our goals.

1. Cheese can be added to any meal. For a _____, try crumbling it over a salad.

2. The cars waited in _____ to get out of the parking lot.

3. Our city has a strong economy. In _____, its neighborhoods are safe and clean.

4. Line up in _____.

5. You've been a doctor for a long time. Why did you decide to go into medicine in the first _____?

6. In the first _____, we don't have enough money. In the second _____, we don't have enough time.

addition
conclusion
end
line
order
place
point
start
sum

7. In _____, everyone agrees that something must be done to preserve the old building.

8. The government spent millions of dollars on the project, but in the _____, officials admitted that the results were not worth the money spent.

9. At this _____ in the process, we should hire an expert.

10. In _____, schools all over the nation are suffering from overcrowded conditions, and we must do something to help them.

Exercise 2

Circle the preposition that correctly completes the sentence.

Example: The new store will add jobs to the local economy. _____ addition, it will pay for road improvements in the surrounding area.

      (In)   At   On

1. _____ this point, we must decide whether to postpone the game.

      In   At   On

2. _____ conclusion, we must act now to save the earth for our children's future.

      For   In   At

3. El Sol is a great family restaurant. _____ a start, the prices are affordable.

      In   At   For

4. There were so many customers waiting _____ line that they opened another register.

      at   for   in

5. I couldn't find the library book I was looking for because it was _____ order.

      at   out of   out

6. Even though we had the materials, our project failed _____ the end because we couldn't find volunteer workers.

      for   on   in

7. We have to know how to cure diseases, but we also have to know how to prevent them _____ the first place.

      at   in   for

8. _____ sum, the politician won the election because of his promise to rebuild the city center.

      At   On   In

Exercise 3

Rewrite the sentences, replacing the underlined part with an idiomatic prepositional phrase.

Example: To summarize, this is the same product but with a new name.
In sum, this is the same product but with a new name.

1. As my final point, I'd like to urge you all to attend tonight's debate.

_____

2. The files are not in sequence.

_____

3. The dean denied the students' requests. Additionally, he barred them from attending faculty meetings.

_____

4. There's a lot to do in Orlando. First, there's Disney World.

_____

5. They will take no further action at this time.

_____

6. The fans stood in a row outside the ticket booth.

_____

7. We shouldn't blame Lloyd for the failure. First, financial predictions are hard to make. Second, we persuaded him to take a job he didn't want.

_____

_____

8. The students are listed in sequence according to their last names.

_____

Exercise 4

The Fremont City Council has proposed changing Oak Street from a two-way street to a one-way street. Mr. Raymond Kruger, who lives on Oak Street, is upset about this proposal. Read his letter to the editor; then answer the questions about it in full sentences.

> Dear Editor,
>
> I am writing to protest against the proposal to change Oak Street from a two-way street to a one-way street. This change would hurt many of us who live on or near Oak Street. For a start, if we have a one-way street, parking would be prohibited on the north side of the street. At this point in time, residents in the Oak Street neighborhood park on both sides of the street. Where would half of the cars be parked?
>
> In addition, many of us would have to go out of our way to get to the main thoroughfare. I imagine that we'd all have to wait in line at Dale Avenue to make a left turn.
>
> But worse than the inconvenience it would cause, a one-way street would ruin the neighborly feel of Oak Street. In the first place, cars would go faster because they would be able to pass slower drivers. And fast cars might hit children crossing the street to visit their friends. In the second place, when cars go fast, they are noisy. Oak Street has always been a quiet street, and I would like to keep it that way.
>
> I urge our council members to consider the problems I mentioned. They will outweigh any advantages to bringing more traffic to the downtown area. In the end, wouldn't everyone be happier if we preserved our small town, where we could live life at a slower pace?
>
> Sincerely,
> Raymond Kruger

Example: Why does Mr. Kruger oppose the council's proposal?
<u>For a start, he believes that if they have a one-way street,</u>
<u>parking would be prohibited on the north side of the street.</u>

1. Where do residents currently park their cars?

   _____

2. Are there any other reasons Mr. Kruger opposes the proposal?

   _____

3. If Oak Street becomes a one-way street, what will residents have to do to get to the main thoroughfare?

   _____

4. Why does Mr. Kruger believe that a one-way street would ruin the neighborly feel of Oak Street?

   _____

Unit C3: Buying and Selling

by check: *using a form that draws money from a bank account*
   We'd like to pay by check, please.
   Did you make your payment by check or credit card?

by credit card: *using a plastic card to buy items on credit*
   I paid for the coat by credit card.
   We can now pay for gas at the gas pump by credit card.

for free: *without charging or being charged any fee*
   He did the work for free.
   I got the car washed for free.

for nothing: *without charging or being charged any fee*
   She catered the party for nothing.
   We got a couch for practically nothing at the garage sale.

for rent: *to be used, but not bought, in exchange for regular payments*
   There are power tools for rent at the hardware store.
   Do you have any apartments for rent?

for sale: *offered for purchase*
   There is a house for sale on the corner.
   Our car is for sale.

in cash: *in bills and coins*
   I have only twenty dollars in cash.
   The sellers want us to pay in cash.

in/out of stock: *available/unavailable for purchase*
   They don't have wool sweaters in stock during the summer.
   Shovels are temporarily out of stock because of the blizzard.

on line: *using a computer*
   We bought our plane tickets on line.
   They sold used cars on line.

on sale: *offered or bought at a discounted price*
   In January, everything in the electronics department will go on sale.
   I bought this coat on sale.

Exercise 1

Choose a word from the box to complete each prepositional phrase below.

Example: Many mail-order companies have put their catalogs on <u>line</u>.

1. He didn't have any cash, so he paid by
   _____.

2. I can't afford this television at this price.
   Will it ever go on _____?

3. That store has Christmas ornaments in
   _____ even during the
   summer.

4. My credit card wasn't accepted, so I paid for
   my new shoes in _____.

5. Our landlord has asked us to move.
   Do you know of any apartments for
   _____?

6. Their house has been for _____ for a long time. They
   can't find any buyers.

7. The company fixed my computer for _____ because it
   was under warranty.

8. She has a big debt because she pays for everything by
   _____.

9. We were able to buy some new software on _____.

10. I did the work for _____ because I owed him a favor.

> cash
> check
> credit card
> free
> line
> nothing
> rent
> sale
> stock

Exercise 2

Circle the preposition that correctly completes the sentence.

Example: Our souvenir mugs are _____ stock right now.

   for   by   (out of)

1. You can buy almost anything _____ credit card.

   in   by   for

2. Winter jackets usually go _____ sale in March.

   for   on   at

3. Is it all right if I pay _____ check?

   for   in   by

4. Sometimes they have used bicycles _____ sale.

   out of   for   in

5. If you buy ten cups of coffee, you get an eleventh cup _____ free.

   in   out of   for

6. I don't have $500 _____ cash right now. Would you accept a check?

   for   on   in

7. They don't have any cabins _____ rent.

   at   in   for

8. We pay many of our bills _____ line.

   for   on   in

Exercise 3

Rewrite the sentences, replacing the underlined part with an idiomatic prepositional phrase.

Example: Louis mowed the old man's lawn <u>without charging anything</u>.
<u>Louis mowed the old man's lawn for nothing.</u>

1. We don't have any printer ribbons <u>available</u> right now.

   _____

2. They bought their dining-room table <u>at a discounted price</u>.

   _____

3. He has $15 <u>in bills and coins</u>.

   _____

4. There will be T-shirts <u>offered for purchase</u> after the concert.

   _____

5. They were moving, so they gave us their old couch <u>without charging us anything</u>.

   _____

6. We couldn't pay <u>by using our credit card</u>, so we had to pay <u>by using cash</u>.

   _____

7. Because of the hot summer, fans were <u>unavailable for purchase</u> by the second week in July.

   _____

8. You can pay <u>by using a check</u>.

   _____

Exercise 4

Trek Sporting Goods has started an advertising campaign to reach as many customers as possible. Read the advertisement; then answer the questions about it.

Trek Sporting Goods
WE SPECIALIZE IN HELPING YOU EXPLORE THE OUTDOORS.

All items carry two-year warranties. Everything replaced at no charge. Simple repairs are also done at no charge unless the problem is due to misuse.

FOR RENT OR FOR SALE
tents, backpacks, mountain bikes, canoes, kayaks, hiking gear

ON SALE
weather radios
Buy one and get one free.

Order Anytime: 1-800-422-2341 or **www.treksport.com**
Payments: Check or credit card. Please do not send cash.

Example: What are some of the items for sale at Trek Sporting Goods?
<u>There are tents, backpacks, and mountain bikes for sale at Trek Sporting Goods.</u>

1. What are some of the items for rent at Trek Sporting Goods?

   _____

2. If your backpack rips after you use it for two months, how much will it cost to replace?

   _____

3. How much do repairs cost during the warranty period?

   _____

4. What's on sale at Trek Sporting Goods?

   _____

5. If you want to order a tent on line, what should you do?

   _____

6. How are payments made on items purchased from Trek Sporting Goods?

   _____

Unit C4: Similarities and Differences

at odds: *in disagreement*

The two countries are at odds.

He doesn't see that the two policies are at odds.

by comparison

This phrase indicates a contrast.

She was so brilliant that the rest of us seemed like idiots by comparison.

in common: *sharing similar features or interests*

The two young boys have a lot in common.

The two proposals have much in common.

in contrast

This phrase indicates a dissimilarity.

Populations of southern cities grew. In contrast, those of northern cities diminished.

in every/no way, in some/many ways

These phrases indicate the extent to which a claim is true.

They were similar in many ways.

in the same way: *likewise*

I learned to swim by practicing; I learned French in the same way.

on the contrary

This phrase introduces a claim while implying that a previously mentioned claim is untrue.

She said few people discuss politics. On the contrary, I discuss it often.

on the one hand

This phrase introduces the first of two contrasting statements. It should be followed by "on the other hand."

On the one hand, the company has always done this. On the other hand, the employees continually complain about the operating policy.

on the other hand

This phrase introduces the second of two contrasting statements. It does not have to be preceded by "on the one hand."

Businesses must earn a profit. On the other hand, they must pay taxes.

to the contrary: *showing the opposite to be true*

Is there any evidence to the contrary?

Exercise 1

Choose a word from the box to complete each prepositional phrase below.

Example: His beliefs and his behavior are at <u>odds</u>.

1. Most students in the United States learn foreign languages when they are in high school.
In _____, citizens of North Carolina begin their language training in elementary school.

2. We fell in love because we had a lot in _____.

3. The two Internet browsers are similar in many _____.

4. Her first novel was a bestseller; by _____, her later books have been disappointing.

5. We have to believe the report: No one has found data to the _____.

6. Some of you might think these ideas are original. On the _____, if you look at the writings of Aristotle, you will find the same claims.

7. It's a hard decision to make. On the one _____, we like convenience. On the other _____, we don't want to pollute the air.

8. You might want to apply for that job. On the other _____, you might not want to if you don't like commuting long distances.

9. Children often imitate bad language they hear on the playground. In the same _____, they often mimic bad language they hear on television.

10. Democrats and Republicans are usually at _____.

common
comparison
contrary
contrast
hand
odds
way
ways

Exercise 2

Circle the preposition that correctly completes the sentence.

Example: What do they have _____ common?

    by   (in)   to

1. _____ some ways, you are right.

    By   On   In

2. He is so industrious that we seem lazy _____ comparison.

    at   by   to

3. Why are they _____ odds?

    at   in   on

4. My younger sister hasn't been very lucky; my younger brother, _____ contrast, has been extremely fortunate.

    at   in   on

5. She might be a good candidate. _____ the one hand, she's very bright.

    On   In   At

6. Rock climbing is a very exciting sport. _____ the other hand, it is also a dangerous one.

    By   In   On

7. She resembles her mother _____ every way.

    by   in   on

8. Is there any information _____ the contrary?

    to   in   on

Exercise 3

Rewrite the sentences, replacing the underlined part with an idiomatic prepositional phrase.

Example: To a great extent, the two are very similar.
In many ways, the two are very similar.

1. They are not at all related.

   _____

2. We are in disagreement.

   _____

3. They had nothing of shared interest.

   _____

4. They were told I spoke fluent Spanish. This is not true. I hardly speak any Spanish.

   _____

5. He published a statement claiming the opposite.

   _____

6. We might be able to win the game tonight. For one thing, we have two home-run hitters. However, one of them is ill.

   _____

7. Children begin to speak when they reach a certain point in their development. Likewise, they begin to read when they are developmentally ready.

   _____

8. There are many old buildings in Eastern cities. Very differently, the skylines of Western cities include very few old buildings.

   _____

Exercise 4

The Campus International Club is discussing plans for its annual International Day. David has proposed changes to the usual schedule of events. Xiaoying doesn't like the proposed changes and prefers to use the original plan. Read over both plans; then answer the questions about them.

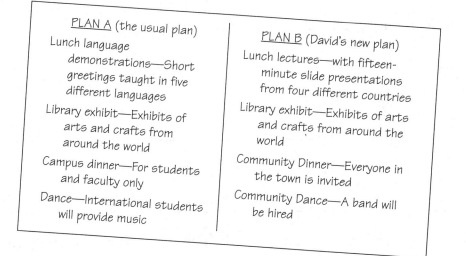

PLAN A (the usual plan)

Lunch language demonstrations—Short greetings taught in five different languages

Library exhibit—Exhibits of arts and crafts from around the world

Campus dinner—For students and faculty only

Dance—International students will provide music

PLAN B (David's new plan)

Lunch lectures—with fifteen-minute slide presentations from four different countries

Library exhibit—Exhibits of arts and crafts from around the world

Community Dinner—Everyone in the town is invited

Community Dance—A band will be hired

Example: Who is at odds with regard to the plans for International Day?
<u>David and Xiaoying are at odds.</u>

1. Do the two plans have anything in common?

_____

2. How are the two dinner plans different?

_____

3. Is it true that Xiaoying wants to have lunch lectures?

_____

4. In the past, International Day has been a small event. What will the day be like with David's plan by comparison?

_____

5. In what ways are the library plans similar?

_____

Unit C5: Health

in good/poor health: *healthy or not healthy*
    I hope everyone in your family is in good health.
    He's been in poor health since his stroke two years ago.

in high/low spirits: *cheerful or not cheerful*
    Although he has to stay in the hospital, he is in high spirits.
    She's been sick for a long time, so she is probably in low spirits.

in pain: *experiencing pain*
    After the accident, he was in pain for weeks.
    Is she in a lot of pain?

in/out of shape: *physically fit or not physically fit*
    I have to get in shape for the race next month.
    He's so out of shape that he can barely climb the stairs.

in therapy: *undergoing treatment for mental or physical illness*
    In therapy, he regained the use of the hand he had damaged.
    My friend's in therapy right now.

on a diet: *adjusting one's food intake, usually in order to lose weight*
    I'm on a diet. I want to lose ten pounds.
    His doctor put him on a diet.

on medication: *taking medicine to treat an illness*
    He's not on any medication right now.
    What medication are you on?

on the mend (informal): *recovering from an injury or illness*
    He could barely move after the accident, but he's on the mend now.
    I'm on the mend. I hope to be back to work by next week.

out of breath: *breathing with difficulty*
    He was out of breath after walking only a short distance.
    I get out of breath very easily when I hike at high altitudes.

under the weather: *feeling slightly ill*
    She didn't go to work because she was feeling under the weather.
    I haven't been sick all winter, but I feel a bit under the weather today.

Exercise 1

Choose a word from the box to complete each prepositional phrase below.

Example: They have been in low <u>spirits</u> since their grandfather became ill.

1. I'm feeling under the _____,
   so I won't be in the office today.

2. Louise is very thin because she's always on a
   _____.

3. He hasn't been in good
   _____ for a long time.

4. Why are you in such low
   _____?

5. I was in so much _____
   that I couldn't sleep.

6. In order to get in _____, he
   started to exercise.

7. I'm on _____ for a sore
   throat, but it makes me dizzy.

8. She had just run three miles, so she was out of _____.

9. Her daughter has been in _____ for two years.

10. I wasn't sure I would recover, but I'm on the _____
    now.

breath

diet

health

medication

the mend

pain

shape

spirits

therapy

weather

Exercise 2

Circle the preposition that correctly completes the sentence.

Example: Grandma is _____ good health for her age.

under   (in)   on

1. Is Brian _____ shape for the marathon?

under   on   in

2. I should go _____ a diet.

on   in   under

3. You should stay home if you're _____ the weather.

under   in   on

4. After I slipped on the ice, I was _____ pain for hours.

out of   in   on

5. Mr. Ellman was dizzy and _____ breath this morning, so we took him to see a doctor.

out of   in   on

6. She's _____ high spirits, even though she has a very bad illness.

under   in   on

7. He's _____ medication for depression.

by   in   on

8. Some of the patients _____ therapy were using weight machines.

to   in   on

Exercise 3

Rewrite the sentences, replacing the underlined part with an idiomatic prepositional phrase.

Example: You look pale. Are you feeling <u>bad</u>?
                <u>You look pale. Are you feeling under the weather?</u>

1. Many people in the region are <u>not healthy</u>.

   _____

2. He is <u>cheerful</u> because he found out he can leave the hospital tomorrow.

   _____

3. The doctor said I was <u>not physically fit</u>.

   _____

4. The patient was <u>experiencing pain</u>, so he was given ibuprofen.

   _____

5. We're happy to know that you're <u>recovering from your illness</u>.

   _____

6. I don't know why I am <u>having difficulty breathing</u>.

   _____

7. Are you <u>eating less</u>? You look thinner.

   _____

8. What are you <u>taking medicine</u> for?

   _____

Exercise 4

Hi-Tech Industries has just opened a company wellness clinic for employees. Read the clinic's first newsletter; then answer the questions about it.

> ## Hi-Tech Wellness Clinic
>
> Dear Hi-Tech Employee,
>
> We're in high spirits here at the Wellness Clinic because we have programs and equipment to help you. If you want to get in shape or stay in shape, we have aerobics classes and exercise machines. If you want to go on a diet, we have a nutritionist for you to consult. We also have counselors for people who would like help with personal issues.
>
> Whether you're in good or poor health, please stop by the clinic.
>
> Sincerely,
>
> Wellness Clinic Staff

Example: Who is in high spirits?
<u>The Wellness Clinic Staff is in high spirits.</u>

1. Why is the Wellness Clinic Staff in high spirits?

   _____

2. Who are the aerobics classes for?

   _____

3. Who might want to use exercise machines?

   _____

4. Who might want to consult a nutritionist?

   _____

5. Who can an employee in low spirits talk to?

   _____

6. Do employees have to be in poor health to stop by the clinic?

   _____

Unit C6: Entertainment

for breakfast/lunch/dinner: *in order to have breakfast/lunch/dinner*
We went to a Greek restaurant for dinner.
On Sundays, we go out for breakfast.

for fun: *for enjoyment and not for any serious reason*
For fun, the teachers dressed up for Halloween.
He's too serious. He never does anything just for fun.

in concert: *giving a live performance*
They saw the Beatles in concert.
I have a CD of Ella in concert.

in suspense: *anticipating something*
We're all in suspense because we won't see the final installment until next week.
The director was good at keeping the audience in suspense.

in/out of town: *performing in/outside the city of one's residence*
My favorite jazz musician is in town.
The Mets are out of town this weekend.

on a tour (of somewhere): *making an organized visit*
We went on a tour of a winery.
Right now they are on a tour of historic sites in the South.

on television/TV: *broadcast as a television program*
There's a funny movie on TV tonight.
We're going to watch the World Cup on television

on the radio: *broadcast as a radio program*
They listened to the baseball game on the radio.
On Saturday afternoons, I listen to a talk show on the radio.

on the town: *visiting several places of entertainment in a city center*
Because of our night on the town, we're tired this morning.
Let's go out on the town!

on vacation: *experiencing a time without work obligations*
I can't wait to be on vacation.
They went on vacation to the Gulf Coast.

Exercise 1

Choose a word from the box to complete each prepositional phrase below.

Example: We met at a neighborhood diner for <u>lunch</u>.

1. She wrote successful thrillers because she was able to keep her readers in _____.

2. The director of the movie was interviewed on the _____ this morning.

3. I'd like to go on a _____ of that old castle.

4. Are the Raiders playing in _____ this Sunday?

5. For _____, we went roller-blading with our kids.

6. The Swing Quartet is in _____ at the Canyon on Saturday.

7. How was your night on the _____?

8. We were on _____ for two weeks.

9. Let's go to Ray's for _____.

10. We watched a documentary on _____ last night.

concert

fun

lunch

radio

suspense

television

tour

town

vacation

Exercise 2

Circle the preposition that correctly completes the sentence.

Example: The tourists went _____ a walking tour of San Francisco.

      in   at   (on)

1. _____ fun, let's go someplace we haven't been before.

      In   For   On

2. I first heard that group _____ the radio.

      for   on   out of

3. We were invited to the Swansons' house _____ dinner.

      in   on   for

4. My brother heard the Rolling Stones _____ concert last summer.

      at   on   in

5. To celebrate, we're going out _____ the town.

      in   on   for

6. We were _____ suspense until the sequel came out.

      for   on   in

7. My son is excited because there's a circus _____ town.

      at   in   for

8. We will be _____ vacation until October 23.

      at   on   in

Exercise 3

Match prepositions to their noun phrases; then complete each sentence with an idiomatic prepositional phrase.

for ——————— dinner
in ————————— fun
on concert
out of town
a tour
suspense
television
the radio
vacation

Example: The fans are happy because the team is playing <u>in town</u> tonight.

1. I bought her CD after I heard her sing _____.

2. I'm tired of eating at home. Let's go out _____ tonight.

3. We're staying home because our team is playing _____ today.

4. What is that strange music _____?

5. The mystery writer held her readers _____ chapter after chapter.

6. You won't be able to reach him because he's _____.

7. _____, we decided to have a costume party. Everyone had a great time.

8. Aaron stayed home from work to watch the World Cup _____.

Exercise 4

Greta and Scott are visiting Seattle for a couple of days. Read their itinerary below and answer the questions about it.

```
Saturday

8:00 A.M.    Breakfast in Pike Place
             Market                          Sunday
10:00 A.M.   Shop                   8:00 A.M.    Breakfast at Seattle Center
12:00 P.M.   Lunch in Pioneer Square 10:00 A.M.  Go up the Space Needle
2:00 P.M.    Mariners baseball game  10:30 A.M.  Visit the amusement park
             at the King Dome        12:30 P.M.  Lunch downtown
6:00 P.M.    Dinner at the pier      1:30 P.M.   Visit the Seattle Art
8:00 P.M.    Mel Corley at Jazz Alley            Museum
                                     6:00 P.M.   Dinner at the Fish Bar
```

Example: Who is on vacation in Seattle?
               <u>Greta and Scott are on vacation in Seattle.</u>

1. Where are Greta and Scott going for breakfast on Saturday morning?

   _____

2. Which sports team is in town this week?

   _____

3. Who are Greta and Scott going to hear in concert?

   _____

4. What are Greta and Scott going to do for fun on Sunday morning?

   _____

5. Where could Greta and Scott go on a tour Sunday afternoon?

   _____

6. Where are Greta and Scott going for dinner on Sunday evening?

   _____

Unit C7: Perspectives

as a matter of fact
> *This phrase introduces detail for, or modification of, a previous statement.*
> As a matter of fact, I'm not studying the Renaissance; I'm studying the Reformation.

beside the point: *irrelevant*
> Ben's comment on the work environment was beside the point in our discussion of work schedules.

for the record
> *This phrase indicates that a statement should be officially recorded.*
> For the record, I vote against this measure.

from someone's perspective
> *This phrase emphasizes that a statement is someone's opinion.*
> From my perspective, public education has improved.

in fact
> *This phrase introduces details that support or contradict a previous statement.*
> The country is thought to be poor, but, in fact, it has many resources.

in/into/out of perspective
> *This phrase indicates the level of importance something has been or should be assigned, relative to other things.*
> He had a hard time keeping his job in perspective.

in someone's opinion
> *This phrase emphasizes that a statement is someone's opinion.*
> In my opinion, this is the best movie of the year.

in someone's view
> *This phrase emphasizes that a statement is someone's opinion.*
> In his view, I was making a big mistake.

of course: *naturally (implied is that the listener is not surprised by the comment)*
> His ideas have had a profound effect on the art world, of course.

off the record
> *This phrase signals that someone does not want a statement published.*
> Off the record, I think he has no chance of winning the election.

Exercise 1

Choose a word from the box to complete each prepositional phrase below.

Example: In my <u>opinion</u>, the process could be made simpler.

1. Because she was afraid of losing her job, she requested that her comment be off the _____.

2. In their _____, we did everything wrong.

3. That's beside the _____. Let's return to our original topic.

4. The teacher helped us put our problems into _____.

course
fact
opinion
perspective
point
record
view

5. Of _____, we have to be careful.

6. The city has been growing rapidly. In _____, its population has doubled in ten years.

7. From my _____, the proposed park would benefit the community.

8. I would like to state for the _____ that I am opposed to this policy.

9. As a matter of _____, he was born in North Dakota, not South Dakota.

10. In my _____, the software should be upgraded.

Exercise 2

Circle the preposition that correctly completes the sentence.

Example: _____ course, the deadline is in three weeks.

     (Of)   In   For

1. _____ the record, I believe he is doing something illegal.

     Off   As   In

2. Let's try to put this situation _____ perspective.

     from   into   of

3. _____ my view, the company should be moved to a bigger city.

     On   In   For

4. She is very generous. _____ fact, she gave $3,000 to the library.

     As   In   On

5. His concern is important but _____ the point.

     beside   in   from

6. _____ her opinion, we should all work ten hours a day.

     From   In   On

7. _____ the record, several of us were concerned about this decision.

     For   In   At

8. You thought he would be elected. Well, _____ a matter of fact, you were right.

     as   in   on

Exercise 3

Match prepositions to their noun phrases; then complete each sentence with an idiomatic prepositional phrase.

as	course
beside	the record
from	perspective
in	a matter of fact
into	someone's perspective
of	fact
off	someone's opinion
	someone's view
	the point

Example: <u>In my opinion</u>, the immigration policy should be reviewed.

1. He is a hard worker. _____, he has a full-time job during the day and takes classes at night.

2. The journalist couldn't report her source because the information had been given _____.

3. _____, he was destined to be a star. They didn't care what anyone else thought.

4. _____, they won't arrive until late at night. Did you expect otherwise?

5. _____, Ms. Murphy should be re-elected because she has a powerful position in the Senate. What do you think?

6. The assignment seemed simple, but _____, it was quite difficult.

7. Your idea is a good one, but it's _____. It has nothing to do with the purpose of this meeting.

8. Once we put the problem _____, it was easier to solve.

Exercise 4

At a local community college, a student committee discusses a proposal to require all school work to be done on computers. Read the excerpt from the discussion below; then answer the questions about it.

SANDRA: In my opinion, the proposal to require all school work to be done on computers is unrealistic. Many of my friends do not have computers at home. In fact, they often have to stay on campus late to finish computer work. Sometimes they have to wait for a computer because there aren't enough computers for everyone.

FRANCIS: I agree. I think the designers of this policy need to put their proposal into perspective. Of course, students need to be computer literate, but the proponents of the policy have to remember what students can afford.

MIKE: I'm about to graduate. From my perspective, the proposal is a good one. Many employers are hiring graduates who have had a lot of experience with computers. Because of my limited work with computers, I'm not hirable. As a matter of fact, I was told recently during an interview that I should take some computer classes before I continued my job search.

SANDRA: Well, if computers are part of our future, in my view, the college should try to make it possible for students to have easy access to computers.

Example: What is Sandra's opinion of the proposal?
<u>In Sandra's opinion, it is unrealistic.</u>

1. What two statements does Sandra make about her friends' access to computers at home?

   _____

2. What does Francis think the designers of the policy need to do?

   _____

3. What does Francis say about students' need to be computer literate?

   _____

4. What is Mike's perspective on the proposal?

   _____

5. What two statements does Mike make about his hirability?

   _____

6. In Sandra's view, what should the college do?

   _____

Unit C8: Process

at the point of doing something: *about to do something*
> We were at the point of announcing our discovery when another team announced the same findings.
> I am at the point of quitting my job because I hate it so much.

by means of something: *using a particular method, process, or tool*
> The pyramids were built by means of slave labor.
> By means of persistence, he became a successful attorney.

in pursuit of something: *attempting to achieve a result*
> He was in pursuit of a big promotion.
> She was in pursuit of success regardless of its cost.

in search of something: *looking for something*
> They left their countries in search of better opportunities.
> The medical team is in search of a cure for the deadly disease.

in the course of something: *during something*
> In the course of our conversation, I realized he had been lying.
> In the course of her career, she learned to tolerate conflict.

in the middle of something: *doing something*
> He was in the middle of a phone conversation when the doorbell rang.
> I am in the middle of a very important project.

in the process of doing something: *currently doing something*
> We are in the process of electing a new chair.
> He is in the process of changing jobs.

on the road to something: *likely to achieve something*
> With that talent, the team is on the road to success.
> The bill passed the House and is on the road to passing the Senate.

on the verge of something: *something is likely to happen soon*
> We were on the verge of a discovery.
> The two countries were on the verge of war.

prior to something: *before something or some point in time*
> Prior to 1964, he was unknown.
> Is there anything we need to do prior to the inspection?

Exercise 1

Choose a word from the box to complete each prepositional phrase below.

Example: They are in <u>pursuit</u> of life, liberty, and happiness.

1. She was at the _____ of calling the police because she was so scared.

2. Susie is on the _____ to recovery.

3. He is on the _____ of a nervous breakdown.

4. They are in the _____ of moving.

5. We are in _____ of a solution that will please everyone.

point

process

road

search

verge

Exercise 2

Circle the preposition that correctly completes the sentence.

Example: I'm _____ the point of telling him exactly what I think.

      in   of   (at)

1. We lived in France prior _____ coming here.

      in   of   to

2. I was _____ the middle of doing my homework when you called.

      in   on   of

3. _____ the course of writing his speech, he realized his opinion had changed.

      In   On   Of

4. The two pieces were held together _____ means of a thin wire.

      on   by   in

5. The soccer team is _____ pursuit of its first championship.

      in   on   by

Exercise 3a

Complete the idiomatic prepositional phrases in the sentences below.

Example: She interrupted me <u>in</u> the middle <u>of</u> my speech.

1. He was _____ the point _____ making a comment when the power went out.

2. _____ the course _____ making our plans, we discovered that we needed more money.

3. They are _____ pursuit _____ a better life.

4. After the disaster, the country was _____ the verge _____ collapse.

5. She's _____ the road _____ stardom.

6. They're _____ the process _____ changing the policy.

7. He got sick _____ the middle _____ the game.

8. The police are _____ search _____ a motive for the crime.

9. He became rich _____ means _____ theft and forgery.

Exercise 3b

What common pattern do most of the multiword prepositions in this unit follow?

Exercise 4

Complete each sentence below with the appropriate multiword prepositional phrase.

Example: <u>Prior to</u> their 1975 concert tour, no one had heard of the band.

1. The supervisor is _____ firing her because she's always late.

2. I can't help you now. I'm _____ assisting someone else.

3. The negotiators were _____ an argument.

4. They're _____ becoming criminals.

5. _____ making the film, the director decided to change the script.

6. I learned a lot _____ preparing my final project for the class.

7. They succeeded _____ hard work and dedication.

8. He was _____ a meaningful job.

9. The young writer was _____ fame.

10. She was a waitress _____ being hired as a receptionist.

Exercise 5

Lisa Hampton is in search of a job. Read her application letter below; then answer the questions about it.

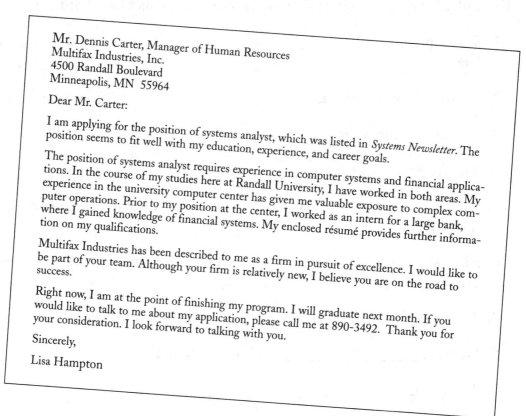

Mr. Dennis Carter, Manager of Human Resources
Multifax Industries, Inc.
4500 Randall Boulevard
Minneapolis, MN 55964

Dear Mr. Carter:

I am applying for the position of systems analyst, which was listed in *Systems Newsletter*. The position seems to fit well with my education, experience, and career goals.

The position of systems analyst requires experience in computer systems and financial applications. In the course of my studies here at Randall University, I have worked in both areas. My experience in the university computer center has given me valuable exposure to complex computer operations. Prior to my position at the center, I worked as an intern for a large bank, where I gained knowledge of financial systems. My enclosed résumé provides further information on my qualifications.

Multifax Industries has been described to me as a firm in pursuit of excellence. I would like to be part of your team. Although your firm is relatively new, I believe you are on the road to success.

Right now, I am at the point of finishing my program. I will graduate next month. If you would like to talk to me about my application, please call me at 890-3492. Thank you for your consideration. I look forward to talking with you.

Sincerely,

Lisa Hampton

Example: What type of a position is Lisa in search of?
<u>She is in search of a job as a systems analyst.</u>

1. What has Lisa gained in the course of her studies?

_____

2. What did Lisa do prior to working at the university computer center?

_____

3. What type of firm is Multifax Industries?

_____

4. Has Lisa already graduated?

_____

Unit C9: Location

across from someone or something: *opposite someone or something*
>The library is across from the cafeteria.
>I sat across from Brad at dinner.

ahead of someone or something: *before someone or something*
>You were ahead of me in line.
>Didn't he see the car ahead of him?

in back of someone or something: *behind someone or something*
>There is a botanical garden in back of Sewell Hall.
>Who sits in back of you in class?

in between some people or some things: *with one person or thing on one side and one on the other*
>I sit in between Pao and Eam.
>Our car is in between yours and the Smiths'.

in front of someone or something: *before someone or something*
>There is a sculpture in front of Barge Hall.
>I gave a speech in front of the class yesterday.

inside (of) something: *within something*
>I'll meet you inside of the entry.
>What's inside the box?

in the middle of something: *in or near the center of something*
>The park is in the middle of town.
>The policeman stood in the middle of the intersection.

next door to someone or something: *beside someone or something*
>I live next door to someone from Guam.
>Their house is next door to the factory.

on top of something: *upon something*
>There's an antenna on top of the roof.
>He always wants a cherry on top of his sundae.

outside (of) something: *external to something*
>They hung a flag outside of the window.
>A stranger was loitering outside the building.

Exercise 1

Choose a word from the box to complete each prepositional phrase below.

Example: The trash cans are in <u>back</u> of the garage.

1. There's a lot of dust on _____ of this bookshelf.

2. Your son's classroom is right next _____ to the cafeteria.

3. The flowers in _____ of the building are beautiful.

4. There is a cow in the _____ of the road.

5. The suitcases are in _____ of the boxes.

back

door

front

middle

top

Exercise 2

Circle the preposition that correctly completes the sentence.

Example: We live across _____ a park.

  in   of   (from)

1. What do you do _____ between classes?

  in   of   on

2. The building right ahead _____ you is the oldest one in the city.

  from   on   of

3. The cats were fighting outside _____ my window.

  in   on   of

4. The animals were kept inside _____ cages.

  on   of   in

5. I put my glasses _____ top of the bureau.

  in   on   from

Exercise 3

Create an idiomatic prepositional phrase with a noun phrase from the box to complete each sentence.

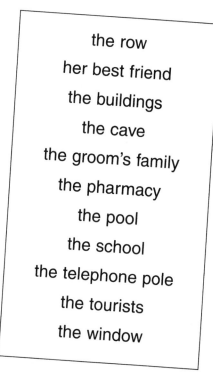

the row
her best friend
the buildings
the cave
the groom's family
the pharmacy
the pool
the school
the telephone pole
the tourists
the window

Example: Our seats were <u>in the middle of the row.</u>

1. The video store is _____.

2. Children were playing _____.

3. There's a walkway _____.

4. At the wedding, we sat _____.

5. Jenny lives _____.

6. There is a bird perched _____.

7. The guide walked _____.

8. She saw someone _____.

9. It was very dark _____.

10. There is a fountain _____.

Exercise 4

Complete these questions with the correct prepositions; then answer the questions, using the words in parentheses.

Example: Who did you sit across <u>from</u>? (Aunt Helen)
<u>I sat across from Aunt Helen.</u>

1. Which building is the weather station on top _____?
(the public library)

_____

2. Who does he live next door _____? (Travis)

_____

3. Who were you sitting in back _____? (Terry)

_____

4. Who were they ahead _____? (the Craigs)

_____

5. Which building were you waiting outside _____?
(the Frost Building)

_____

6. Who did they sit in front _____ at the ceremony?
(their old friends)

_____

7. Which box did he hide inside _____? (the wooden one)

_____

8. Who did she live across _____? (the apartment
superintendent)

_____

Exercise 5

Nicole is writing to her parents, describing her new apartment. Read her letter; then answer the questions about it.

> Dear Mom and Dad,
>
> My new apartment is great! It has a kitchen, living room, bedroom, and bath. The living room is my favorite place to be, so I'm going to try to describe it to you. When you walk into the room, you look out a window at the park I live across from, Viewpoint Park. I have a desk in front of the window. I like to study there. I keep a picture of our family on top of the desk to remind me of home.
>
> In the middle of the room, there are a couple of chairs and a sofa. In back of the sofa, there is a table with a lamp. I prefer to read on the sofa because the chairs are uncomfortable. In front of the sofa, there is a low table. I leave my dictionary on this table, so I can look up words easily. There's a big closet in the living room, too. It is so big that you can walk inside of it.
>
> As you can tell, I'm very happy with my apartment. I hope you can visit me soon. I have to get back to my work now. I'll write more later.
>
> Love,
>
> Nicole

Example: Where does Nicole live?
<u>She lives across from a park.</u>

1. Where does Nicole have her desk?

_____

2. What does Nicole do to remind her of home?

_____

3. Where is the sofa?

_____

4. Where is the lamp?

_____

5. Where is the low table?

_____

6. What is special about Nicole's closet?

_____

Unit C10: Exceptions and Substitutions

apart from something: *excluding someone or something*
Apart from his description of the villain, his story fascinated me.
Apart from doing the laundry, I didn't do much at all today.

except for someone or something: *excluding someone or something*
Everyone signed the petition except for Debbie.
Except for having a flat tire outside Tucson, our trip to Arizona was great.

in lieu of something: *as a substitution for something*
I worked at the charity dinner in lieu of giving a cash donation.
In lieu of having a formal wedding, they decided to get married on the beach.

in place of someone or something: *as a substitution for someone or something*
They served green beans in place of corn at lunch.
In place of the Saxton Quintet, the Rollins Band played the opening song.

in spite of something: *not prevented by something*
We played tennis in spite of the rain.
In spite of her illness, she was always cheerful.

instead of someone or something: *as a substitution for someone or something*
The assistant, instead of the director, met with the new clients.
For dinner tonight let's have pizza instead of meatloaf.

irrespective of something: *not prevented by something*
Everyone has the right to vote, irrespective of race, religion, or gender.
The students were all admitted, irrespective of their ability to pay for classes.

regardless of something: *not influenced by something*
They decided to build the new center regardless of the opposition.
He continued to smoke regardless of the doctor's warning.

save for someone or something: *excluding someone or something*
Everyone was there save for Dr. Sawyer.
All of the seats were filled save for a few in the last row.

with the exception of someone or something: *excluding something*
My day was great with the exception of having to wait in traffic.
With the exception of my sister, everyone was at the family reunion.

Exercise 1

Choose a word from the box to complete each prepositional phrase below.

Example: We used markers in <u>place</u> of paint to make the posters.

1. In _____ of the heavy rain, we drove on to our destination.

2. With the _____ of Barb, everyone arrived on time.

3. In _____ of a raise, the employers offered workers more vacation time.

4. She went to work today in _____ of having a cold.

5. Professor Case used a pencil in _____ of a red pen to correct papers.

> exception
> lieu
> place
> spite

Exercise 2

Circle the preposition that correctly completes the sentence.

Example: Instead _____ finishing her homework, Gina watched television.

      (of)   in   for

1. Regardless _____ the consequences, they quit their jobs.

      with   of   for

2. Apart _____ their closest friends, no one knew they planned to move.

      with   from   of

3. Irrespective _____ our wishes, he hitchhiked from New York to California.

      in   with   of

4. She wore no jewelry save _____ a ring her mother had given her.

      for   of   in

5. You remember everything except _____ my birthday.

      in   on   for

Exercise 3a

List each phrasal preposition under the category that describes it. Which part of speech can be found in three- or four-word phrasal prepositions but not in two-word phrasal prepositions?

Two-Word	*Three- or Four-Word*
_____	_____
_____	_____
_____	_____
_____	_____
_____	_____
_____	_____

Exercise 3b

Complete the idiomatic prepositional phrases in the sentences below.

Example: <u>Save for</u> a few quarters, I have absolutely no money right now.

1. She used skim milk _____ cream in her coffee.

2. _____ their origin, the recent immigrants worked together to improve their English.

3. _____ Wallace, we all passed the exam.

4. I remembered everything _____ an umbrella.

5. They decided to leave _____ the storm warning.

Exercise 4a

Create sentences by combining one item from each of the columns. Start each sentence with an idiomatic prepositional phrase.

telling silly jokes	I like the class
yawning a lot	the professor should tell an exciting story
giving only a final exam	the professor should ask us to write a final paper
speaking softly	my classmates enjoy the course
assigning speeches	the professor should give weekly quizzes
having too much homework	the professor engages the students in discussions
having to give speeches	the professor gives interesting lectures

Example: Apart from telling silly jokes, the professor gives interesting lectures.

1. _____
2. _____
3. _____
4. _____
5. _____
6. _____

Exercise 4b

The object of the preposition in the sentences above is a

_____.

❚ Exercise 5

Cheryl has been asked by the company supervisor to plan a celebration for visitors from the company's overseas plant. Look over her notes below; then answer the supervisor's questions about Cheryl's assignment.

```
Task                    Notes
hotel                   staying at Holiday Inn, Mr. Kim
                        with relatives
invitations             can't find Mr. Hermann's address
tour guide              Ms. Lamont
lunch                   Garden Cafe
meeting                 visitors prefer to meet after lunch
free time               10:30 A.M. – 11:30 A.M. only
dinner                  ?
```

Example: SUPERVISOR: Where are our visitors staying?
CHERYL: <u>With the exception of Mr. Kim</u>, everyone is staying at the Holiday Inn.

1. SUPERVISOR: Has everything been planned?

   CHERYL: _____

2. SUPERVISOR: Has everyone been sent an invitation?

   CHERYL: _____

3. SUPERVISOR: Will Ms. Green be giving the tour?

   CHERYL: _____

4. SUPERVISOR: Have we planned an outdoor picnic?

   CHERYL: _____

5. SUPERVISOR: Would the visitors like to meet in the morning?

   CHERYL: _____

6. SUPERVISOR: Will the visitors have any free time?

   CHERYL: _____

Unit CII: Decisions

as a consequence of something

This phrase introduces the cause of some event, condition, or practice.

The business went bankrupt as a consequence of mismanagement.

as a result of something

This phrase introduces the cause of some event, condition, or practice.

We are suffering financially as a result of the decisions he made.

because of something

This phrase introduces the cause of some event, condition, or practice.

I could afford the tuition because of my aunt and uncle's generosity.

for the sake of something: ***so something can occur or be achieved***

For the sake of peace at the dinner table, they never discussed politics.

Let's imagine for the sake of argument that we did not achieve our goals this year.

in favor of something: ***supporting something***

The senator was not in favor of cutting taxes.

I am in favor of stricter regulations.

in view of something: ***considering something***

In view of the recent information we received, we may want to rethink our decision.

In view of these facts, what should we do?

on account of something: ***because something occurred***

We couldn't go on account of the bad weather.

On account of his decisions, we lost money.

out of respect for someone or something: ***recognizing someone's rights or wishes***

Out of respect for the family, the issue was never discussed in public.

Out of respect for her privacy, we never called her at home.

owing to something

This phrase introduces the cause of some event, condition, or practice.

Owing to a computer breakdown, we were unable to enter the data.

with a view toward something: ***hoping that something will result from the action***

She opened a small business with a view toward expanding it in a few years.

Exercise 1

Choose a word from the box to complete each prepositional phrase below.

Example: In <u>view</u> of the possible consequences, he decided not to discuss the matter with the director.

1. For the _____ of efficiency, I have developed a schedule for us to follow.

2. He was campaigning for Dick Lowry, with a _____ toward becoming a candidate himself in a few years.

3. Out of _____ for their traditional holiday, their boss did not require them to come to work.

4. Is he in _____ of national health care?

5. As a _____ of his procrastination, we're not finished with our work.

favor
respect
result
sake
view

Exercise 2

Circle the preposition that correctly completes the sentence.

Example: He gave his life _____ the sake of his country's independence.

      as   in   (for)

1. _____ view of the possible side effects, I chose not to have the treatment.

      In   With   As

2. She had to cancel the concert because _____ a family emergency.

      with   on   of

3. _____ a consequence of her carelessness, she was fired.

      As   On   In

4. _____ account of your incompetence, we lost the contract.

      In   On   For

Exercise 3

Complete the idiomatic prepositional phrases in the sentences below.

Example: I'm <u>in favor of</u> the ban on assault weapons.

1. _____ a productive meeting, he sent all members an agenda so they could be prepared.

2. _____ our lack of preparation, our presentation was a fiasco.

3. The newlyweds built a small house, _____ adding on rooms when they had children.

4. _____ a poor growing season, food prices will be high this year.

5. _____ these questions, we should not make our decision today.

6. The streams became polluted _____ overdevelopment.

7. _____ your help, I was able to finish by the deadline.

8. They decided to cancel their visit _____ the airline strike.

9. _____ the senior citizens, fees were reduced.

10. They're both _____ the proposed changes to the law.

Exercise 4

Complete these sentences. Create an idiomatic prepositional phrase with a gerund phrase from the box.

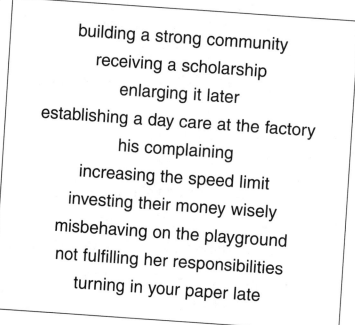

building a strong community
receiving a scholarship
enlarging it later
establishing a day care at the factory
his complaining
increasing the speed limit
investing their money wisely
misbehaving on the playground
not fulfilling her responsibilities
turning in your paper late

Example: There were many accidents <u>as a result of increasing the speed limit</u>.

1. _____, you will receive a lower grade.

2. The Sawyers put in a small garden, _____.

3. _____, we were given more work.

4. I'm _____. There are many working mothers there.

5. He was sent home from school _____.

6. She went to a good school _____.

7. _____, we urge you to attend the town meeting on Monday night.

8. She was fired _____.

9. _____, they were able to retire early.

10. They are not _____ because they are concerned about driver safety.

Exercise 5

Read the headlines below; then answer the questions about them.

> Students Riot, Police Called In
> Sen. Noguchi For New Amendment
> Bad Roads, Many Accidents
> Illegal Activity Exposed, Official Resigns
> Food Shop Now, Restaurant Later
> Storm Warnings, Residents Cautious
> Rain, Game Postponed

Example: Why did an official resign?
An official resigned as a consequence of illegal activity being exposed.

1. Why were there many accidents?

   _____

2. What is Senator Noguchi in favor of?

   _____

3. Why were the police called in?

   _____

4. There is a new businessman in town. Is he opening up a food shop or a restaurant?

   _____

5. Why are the residents being cautious?

   _____

6. Why was the game postponed?

   _____

Unit C12: Reference

as for something
This phrase signals a slight change in subject.
Jodi is very nice. As for her writing skills, she has much to learn.

in case of something: *if something happens*
In case of fire, call 911.
In case of an emergency, call the neighbors.

in keeping with something: *following something*
In keeping with tradition, the company's holiday celebration will be on December 22.
In keeping with the spirit of the day, we invited friends to dinner.

in light of something
This phrase introduces the cause of some event, condition, or practice.
The court reversed its decision in light of new evidence.

in/with reference to something: *about something*
I'm calling in reference to your job posting.
With reference to your article on cats, I was wondering how you measure their speed.

in regard to something: *referring to something*
The company is reviewing its policy in regard to unpaid leave.
In regard to a recent memo, many employees registered complaints.

in relation to something: *connected to something*
I would like to say something in relation to a comment made earlier.
Many questions have been asked in relation to this issue.

in the wake of something: *following something chronologically*
In the wake of the stalled negotiations, the pilots went on strike.
In the wake of the announcement, many people refinanced their homes.

on behalf of someone: *representing a group of people*
He spoke on behalf of the whole student body.
On behalf of my family, I'd like to thank you for your kindness.

with respect to something: *referring to something*
With respect to customer satisfaction, the company has enlarged the customer service department.
The hospital has improved with respect to its outpatient care.

Exercise 1

Choose a word from the box to complete each prepositional phrase below.

Example: On <u>behalf</u> of the citizens, the mayor welcomed the governor.

1. In _____ to your recent request, we wish to inform you that your order has been sent.

2. In the _____ of the election, much new legislation was passed.

3. I am writing with _____ to your advertisement in the *Post*.

4. In _____ of an accident, notify your closest relative.

5. With _____ to the workload, I believe it to be reasonable.

> case
>
> reference
>
> regard
>
> respect
>
> wake

Exercise 2

Circle the preposition that correctly completes the sentence.

Example: _____ respect to your request, we are sending you a refund.

    (With)   On   For

1. Mr. Harvey benefited from the policy. As _____ us, we made no gains.

    with   of   for

2. In light _____ the study, the advertisers discussed a different strategy.

    with   to   of

3. In keeping _____ the wishes of my family, I attended Lincoln College.

    in   with   of

4. I have something to say _____ relation to your topic.

    on   of   in

5. The President honored the soldiers _____ behalf of the nation.

    in   on   with

Exercise 3

Complete the idiomatic prepositional phrases in the sentences below.

Example: <u>With respect to</u> the statistics presented, we believe a company health plan is necessary.

1. The hotel lobby was beautiful. _____ our room, though, it was small and dark.

2. _____ of illness, you should find a substitute.

3. I'm calling _____ your garage sale on Saturday.

4. We asked questions _____ previous decisions.

5. _____ that information, we can now draw some conclusions.

6. I would like to welcome you _____ everyone here.

7. _____ the 1995 study, I would like to mention a few weak points I see.

8. _____ the merger, the company was very disorganized.

9. _____ custom, he bought a huge turkey for Thanksgiving.

10. _____ welfare, he proposed several reforms.

Exercise 4a

Create sentences by combining one item from each of the columns. Start each sentence with an idiomatic prepositional phrase.

what she has argued   I agree

what he stated as fact ————— I disagree

what we have done in the past   I'd like to raise an issue

what they have proposed   I'd like to say a few words

what you have presented   I'd like to ask a question

what they criticized

Example: <u>As for what he stated as fact, I disagree.</u>

1. _____

2. _____

3. _____

4. _____

5. _____

Exercise 4b

The object of the preposition can be a noun phrase; sometimes it can also

be a _____.

Exercise 5

Franklin Delano Roosevelt, the 32nd president of the United States, accomplished much in his four terms. He is admired for the work he did to help all citizens. Below you will see problems that the United States was facing during his presidency, listed with Roosevelt's solutions to them. Read over the list; then answer the questions about it.

Businesses and Farms with Financial Problems
National Recovery Administration

Poor Relations with Latin America
Good Neighbor Policy

Unemployment
Public Works Administration
Works Progress Administration

Poor Elderly People
Social Security

Unemployed and Poor Youth
Civilian Conservation Corps

Underdeveloped Resources
Tennessee Valley Authority

Bombing of Pearl Harbor
Declaration of War

Example: What policy did Roosevelt establish in light of poor relations with Latin America?
In light of poor relations with Latin America, Roosevelt established the Good Neighbor Policy.

1. What agency did Roosevelt establish with respect to businesses in financial trouble?

   _____

2. What did Roosevelt do with regard to unemployed youth?

   _____

3. What did Roosevelt do in regard to underdeveloped resources?

   _____

4. What did Roosevelt do in the wake of the bombing of Pearl Harbor?

   _____

5. What agency did Roosevelt establish in light of severe unemployment?

   _____

D

Verb Phrases

Three types of multiword verb phrases are presented in this section.

- Units D1 through D4 focus on prepositional verb phrases. In these units, you will learn to combine verbs with the prepositions most commonly accompanying them (e.g., *focus on*).

- Units D5 through D11 cover phrasal verbs, which consist of **verb + particle** collocations. Unlike the **verb + preposition** combinations in earlier chapters, **verb + particle** collocations possess meanings that cannot be derived easily from the meaning of the words when they are divided up (e.g., *divide up*). If you have studied phrasal verbs before, you may be familiar with other labels for **particle**. Although "adverb" and "preposition" are sometimes used, **particle** is used here because the words it refers to are distinct from prepositions and other adverbs.

- Unit D12 deals with **phrasal-prepositional verbs**, which are **verb + particle + preposition** collocations (e.g., *find out about*).

Verb phrases in each unit all refer to a specific context and are listed alphabetically. The verb appears first, followed by the most commonly used preposition or particle. If the verb phrase requires an object, a pronoun will be listed (e.g., *someone* or *something*). In Units D5 through D12, definitions are given for each verb phrase, as the meaning may not be immediately apparent. In addition, each phrasal verb is identified in one of the following ways: **I** = Intransitive, **T-Sep** = Transitive (the verb and particle may be *separated*), **T-Sep (OB)** = the separation is *obligatory*, or **T-Insep** = Transitive (the verb and particle are *inseparable*).

Unit D1: Friends

care about someone or something
> I care about my friends.
> He doesn't care about your feelings.

chat/talk with someone
> I chatted with my friend's mother.
> Did you talk with Jeremy yesterday?

gossip about someone or something
> They gossip about everyone.
> Why do you gossip about your friends?

happen to someone or something
> Something terrible happened to Gary.
> What happened to the car?

hear about someone or something
> I heard about the big fight at the party.
> Did you hear about Perla?

know about someone or something
> You know about him, don't you?
> They both knew about cars.

laugh about something
> They laughed about the joke all evening.
> We laughed about the misunderstanding.

live with someone
> Ted lives with his friends.
> She lived with her best friend for two years.

share something with someone
> She shared her lunch with me.
> He shared his tools with his neighbors.

wait for someone or something
> She's waiting for her friend.
> We're anxiously waiting for their reply.

Exercise 1

Fill in the blanks below with the correct verbs.

Example: Doesn't he <u>care</u> about anything?

1. I _____ with two of my friends in an apartment.

2. Do you _____ about the party tonight?

3. I'll _____ with Marta tomorrow.

4. Did you _____ your news with your friends?

5. Did anything bad _____ to her?

happen
know
live
share
talk

Exercise 2

Circle the preposition that correctly completes the sentence.

Example: Did you hear _____ Tammy's award?

(about)   for   with

1. I chatted _____ her on the telephone.

about   for   with

2. Please wait _____ me.

about   for   to

3. Something happened _____ Astrid.

about   for   to

4. They laughed _____ their childhood pranks.

about   for   with

5. We shouldn't gossip _____ Martin.

about   to   for

Exercise 3a

Fill in the blanks below with the correct noun phrase. You will need to supply the correct prepositions.

Example: She gossiped <u>about her best friend.</u>

1. I shared my popcorn _____.

2. Did you hear _____?

3. What happened _____?

4. Because we didn't reach the gate on time, we

   had to wait _____.

5. They sat in the corner and chatted _____.

> Wanda's accident
>
> Alan
>
> your car
>
> each other
>
> another flight

Exercise 3b

Answer the questions below in complete sentences, using the words in parentheses. Remember to change second-person pronouns to first-person pronouns.

Example: Who is she talking with? (her childhood friend)
<u>She is talking with her childhood friend.</u>

1. What does he know about them? (their reputation)

   _____

2. Who does your friend live with? (her parents)

   _____

3. What does she care about? (her pets)

   _____

4. What happened to Julia today? (something wonderful)

   _____

5. What did you hear about Andrés? (his good luck)

   _____

Exercise 4

Read the first sentence; then complete the second sentence with a prepositional verb, using the noun + preposition from the first sentence.

Example: There was a lot of gossip about the event.
They <u>gossiped about</u> the event.

1. I had a long chat with her.

   I _____ her for a long time.

2. We had a good laugh about our childhood.

   We _____ our childhood.

3. The wait for our flight was long.

   We _____ our flight.

4. She had a nice talk with her old friend today.

   She _____ her old friend today.

5. The gossip about my friend wasn't true.

   They _____ my friend.

Exercise 5

Complete these questions with the correct prepositions.

Example: Who do you care <u>about?</u>

1. Who did you share your sandwich _____?

2. What are you laughing _____?

3. Who are you gossiping _____?

4. Who do you live _____?

5. What are you waiting _____?

Exercise 6

Eduardo has just received a letter from some old friends who moved out of the country a couple of years ago. They are worried because Eduardo hasn't written for several months. Read the letter below; then answer the questions about it in full sentences.

Dear Eduardo,

We have been looking for a letter from you in our mailbox, but we haven't found one yet. Please write. We care about you and want to hear about you and your family. We worry that something terrible has happened to you.

We are fine here. Do you remember Lise? She is living with us now, and a friend is sharing an office with her. Yesterday, we were talking with her about our old neighborhood. We laughed about old times.

We would like to see you again. Could you visit soon? We are waiting eagerly for your letter.

Love,

Mina and Jessie

Example: Who do Mina and Jessie care about?
<u>Mina and Jessie care about Eduardo.</u>

1. Who is living with Mina and Jessie?

   _____

2. Who is sharing an office with Lise?

   _____

3. What do Mina and Jessie want to hear about?

   _____

4. What were Mina, Jessie, and their guest laughing about?

   _____

5. What are Mina and Jessie waiting for?

   _____

concentrate on something

> I have to concentrate on my work.
> If you concentrate on the problem, you should find a solution.

focus on something

> The teacher focused on the ideas of the eighteenth century.
> I am focusing on the causes of the Revolutionary War.

learn about someone or something

> We learned about Karl Marx today.
> They learned about jazz in their music class.

lecture on something

> He lectured on the efforts to preserve local forests.
> I will lecture on English idioms.

listen to someone or something

> We listened to a recording of the play.
> Did you listen to your classmates?

read about something

> She read about Canada's political system in the encyclopedia.
> We are going to read about cultural differences.

report on something

> They reported on their work.
> When will you report on the critical events of the century?

talk about something

> The students talked about the assignment.
> The teacher talked about the class requirements.

think of something

> I should think of a topic for my paper.
> He thought of a great idea for our presentation.

write about something

> Did you write about the life of Queen Victoria?
> We wrote about our families.

Exercise 1

Fill in the blanks below with the correct verbs.

Example: In his English paper, he will <u>concentrate</u> on phrasal verbs.

1. In chapter one, you will _____ about Navajo pottery.

2. You need to _____ of a title for your paper.

3. The guest speaker will _____ on El Niño.

4. You can _____ to CDs in the music library.

5. After you finish today, you should

    _____ on your progress.

lecture

listen

read

report

think

Exercise 2

Circle the preposition that correctly completes the sentence.

Example: What did you learn _____ in school today?

     (about)   of   on

1. Which theory did you concentrate _____?

         about   of   on

2. He wrote _____ his experience in China.

         about   for   to

3. She couldn't think _____ the answer.

         about   of   to

4. They talked _____ current events.

         about   of   on

5. My paper focuses _____ the peace treaty.

         of   on   to

Exercise 3a

Check the box next to the sentence that is written correctly.

Example: ⊠ We learned about it yesterday.
⬚ We learned it about yesterday.

1. ⬚ We read it about in the newspaper.
⬚ We read about it in the newspaper.

2. ⬚ They listened to us.
⬚ They listened us to.

3. ⬚ She reported on it.
⬚ She reported it on.

Exercise 3b

Rewrite each sentence, replacing the underlined noun phrase with a pronoun.

Example: We talked about <u>the event</u> in class.
<u>We talked about it in class.</u>

1. She wrote about <u>George Washington Carver.</u>

   _____

2. I didn't listen to <u>my teachers.</u>

   _____

3. The article focuses on <u>the author's wife.</u>

   _____

Exercise 3c

In declarative sentences and yes/no questions, can a pronoun ever separate the verb and the preposition in a prepositional verb?

Exercise 4

Read the first sentence; then complete the second sentence with a prepositional verb, using the noun + preposition from the first sentence.

Example: I went to a lecture on the exploration of Mars.
He <u>lectured on</u> the exploration of Mars.

1. The report on her experiment was interesting.

    She _____ her experiment.

2. Their focus on bilingualism was controversial.

    They _____ bilingualism.

3. He gave a talk about sign language.

    He _____ sign language.

4. Their concentration on the subject was intense.

    They _____ the subject.

5. I will give a lecture on American proverbs.

    I will _____ American proverbs.

Exercise 5

Fill in the blanks below with the correct prepositions.

Example: What are you writing <u>about?</u>

1. How did you think _____ that great idea?

2. Who are they listening _____?

3. What are you learning _____?

4. What will you report _____?

5. What topics can you lecture _____?

Exercise 6

You are looking through a college catalog. Read the course description below; then answer the questions about it in full sentences.

Course Offering: *Culture of the United States*
MWF 11:00–12:00

In this course, students will learn about many aspects of U.S. culture, but the course focuses on music. In class, students listen to many types of music that are currently popular in the United States. The teacher lectures on specific topics on Mondays. On Wednesdays, the class talks about an assigned reading. On Fridays, students report on their own research. At the end of the course, students will write about some type of music that they have studied.

Example: What will students learn about if they take *Culture of the United States*?
<u>Students will learn about many aspects of U.S. culture.</u>

1. What does the course focus on?

_____

2. What do students listen to in class?

_____

3. What happens on Mondays?

_____

4. What does the class do on Wednesdays?

_____

5. What happens on Fridays?

_____

6. What must students do at the end of the course?

_____

Unit D3: Working Together

(dis)agree with someone/about something
> I disagree with you about the plan.
> They agree with each other.

argue with someone/about something
> We never argue with them about money.
> They always argue about schedules.

complain to someone/about someone or something
> You complain to us about everything.
> We complained about the salary.

depend on someone or something (for something)
> We'll depend on you for transportation.
> They depended on her generosity.

rely on someone or something (for something)
> You can rely on me.
> We rely on your letters for information.

side with someone/against someone or something
> They sided with the liberals against the bill.
> Will you side with us?

speak to someone/about something
> You should speak to someone about that.
> She spoke to me yesterday.

talk to someone/about something
> I talked to the boss about my plan.
> Have you talked about it?

unite with someone or something/against someone or something
> We must unite against the unfair practices.
> Most of the workers united with the drivers who were on strike.

work with someone/on something
> We worked with her for sixteen years.
> How many people worked with you on the project?

Exercise 1

Fill in the blanks below with the correct verbs.

Example: We <u>agree</u> with you.

1. Did you _____ about the work assignments?

2. I'll _____ to you tomorrow.

3. He can _____ on the machine at 10:00.

4. My coworkers _____ on me.

5. They'll _____ against management.

argue

depend

side

talk

work

Exercise 2

Circle the preposition that correctly completes the sentence.

Example: I spoke _____ them yesterday.

    about   over   (to)

1. We should unite _____ the other department.

    about   for   with

2. Our friends rely _____ us.

    about   on   to

3. We disagreed _____ our work benefits.

    about   for   to

4. I have worked _____ Chen for six years.

    about   to   with

5. She spoke _____ me yesterday.

    about   to   over

Exercise 3

Fill in the blanks below with the correct prepositions.

Example: They disagreed <u>with</u> us <u>about</u> the plan.

1. She spoke _____ her colleague _____ her concerns.

2. He argued _____ us _____ schedule changes.

3. Side _____ us _____ the layoffs.

4. Can we rely _____ you _____ help?

5. Who will work _____ me _____ this project?

Exercise 4

Read the first sentence; then complete the second sentence with a prepositional verb, using the noun + preposition from the first sentence.

Example: Her coworker's dependence on her makes her feel important.
Her coworker <u>depends on</u> her.

1. His reliance on his colleagues for support was not unreasonable.

   He _____ his colleagues for support.

2. Her complaint to the supervisor was ignored.

   She _____ the supervisor.

3. Their disagreement about the plans for the new building lasted two months.

   They _____ the plans for the new building.

4. Let's have a short talk about today's schedule.

   Let's _____ today's schedule.

5. They had a big argument about productivity.

   They _____ productivity.

Exercise 5

Answer the questions below, using the words in parentheses. Remember to change second-person pronouns to first-person pronouns.

Example: What do you depend on your friend for?   (advice)
<u>I depend on my friend for advice.</u>

1. Who do you depend on for help?   (my friend)

   _____

2. What did she complain to the manager about?   (her salary)

   _____

3. Who did she complain to about her salary?   (the manager)

   _____

4. Which project did you work with him on?   (the marketing project)

   _____

Exercise 6

The order of some prepositional phrases may be reversed. Rewrite the following sentences, exchanging the positions of the prepositional phrases.

Example: They worked with the committee on the budget.
<u>They worked on the budget with the committee.</u>

1. They talked to the director about their work.

   _____

2. We argued about employee benefits with management.

   _____

3. The workers spoke to a union representative about their jobs.

   _____

4. I worked on the design with Merlin.

   _____

Exercise 7

Vochi has been offered a new job, but she isn't sure she wants to take it because she likes many things about her current position. To help make the decision, she has written a list of the positive and negative things about her job. Her decision to accept the job offer or not will be based on this list. Read through Vochi's list; then answer the questions about it in full sentences.

Positives	Negatives
• My coworkers and I agree about our goals. • We work on projects together. • We talk to one another about problems. • My office mate and I depend on each other.	• My coworkers and I disagree about office assignments. • We can't speak to the supervisor about our concerns. • We argue about our duties. • I don't like Vern because he always complains about the rest of us to the supervisor.

Example: What do Vochi and her coworkers agree about?
<u>They agree about their goals.</u>

1. What do Vochi and her coworkers argue about?

   _____

2. Can Vochi speak to her supervisor about her concerns?

   _____

3. Why doesn't Vochi like Vern?

   _____

4. What do Vochi and her coworkers do together?

   _____

5. What do Vochi and her coworkers disagree about?

   _____

Unit D4: Shopping

ask for something

We asked for assistance.

Did you ask for help?

beg for something

The child begged for ice cream.

A man outside the shop begged for money.

glance at something

I glanced at the gloves while I was waiting for you.

He glanced at the sign to see if the store was open.

laugh at something

The children laughed at the clowns in the square.

She laughed at my new wild-colored tie.

look at something

I was looking at dresses today.

He was looking at joke books.

look for something

Are you looking for anything special?

I'm looking for a gift for my friend.

point at something

The toddler pointed at the lollipops.

Because I couldn't speak French, I just pointed at the fruit I wanted.

search for something

I searched for my passport.

They searched for an original copy in the antiquarian bookstore.

shop for something

She's shopping for shoes today.

I shopped for groceries yesterday.

stare at someone or something

The little boy stared at the toy trains in the window.

She stared at herself in the mirror.

Exercise 1

Fill in the blanks below with the correct verbs.

Example: <u>Point</u> at the one you want.

1. I usually _____ for clothes at the mall.

2. Did you _____ at any new cars?

3. We didn't have much time, so I could only

   _____ at the watches on sale.

4. If you don't know where the store is, why don't you

   _____ for directions?

5. You can _____ for your
   lost mittens in the lost-and-found box.

ask

glance

look

search

shop

Exercise 2

Circle the prepositional phrase that correctly completes the sentence.

Example: The clerk asked _____.

at my credit card   for my credit card

1. She pointed _____.

   at the price   for the price

2. We were laughing _____.

   at the funny T-shirt   for the funny T-shirt

3. I practically begged _____, but still no one would assist me.

   at help   for help

4. The number of books amazed him. He could only stare _____.

   at them   for them

Exercise 3a

Place the verbs under the preposition they precede.
One verb will appear in both columns.

at	for
_____	_____
_____	_____
_____	_____
_____	_____
_____	_____

ask
beg
glance
laugh
look
point
search
shop
stare

Exercise 3b

When combined with the verbs in this unit, what does *at* imply?

When combined with the verbs in this unit, what does *for* imply?

Exercise 4

Answer the questions below in complete sentences, using the words in parentheses. Remember to change second-person pronouns to first-person pronouns.

Example: Did you have time to glance at anything?   (some new CDs)
<u>I had time to glance at some new CDs.</u>

1. What are you laughing at?   (these funny ties)

   _____

2. Are you looking for anything in particular?   (long-sleeved T-shirts)

   _____

3. What did you ask the clerk for?   (my receipt)

   _____

4. Which watch are you pointing at?   (the silver one)

   _____

Exercise 5

Read the first sentence; then complete the response with a clause including a verb + preposition. Remember to change first-person pronouns to second-person pronouns.

Example: I'm searching for my credit card.
The credit card <u>you're searching for</u> is on the counter.

1. My daughter has been begging for that dinosaur puzzle in your store window.

   The dinosaur puzzle _____
   is no longer in the window. It has been sold.

2. We're looking for a French bakery.

   The bakery _____
   is right around the corner.

3. I was looking at a winter coat.

   The winter coat _____
   costs $500.

4. He asked for a cellular phone.

   He received the cellular phone _____.

5. She was shopping for a special gift.

   She found the special gift _____.

Exercise 6

Read the shopping advertisements; then answer the questions about them in full sentences.

MARK'S SPORTING GOODS *We specialize in golf and tennis* *Check our sale bin for old or used tennis rackets.*	**LUNDY'S** **Shoes for the whole family** **Sale on Sneakers this week**	*Jamaica's High Fashion* Look great from head to foot Shoes for Special Occasions

Example: Where did Kenji search for tennis rackets that aren't made anymore?
<u>He searched for tennis rackets that aren't made anymore at Mark's Sporting Goods.</u>

1. Where should Eva shop for sandals for her son?

   _____

2. Where should Ming look for a cheap pair of sneakers?

   _____

3. Where should Ann ask for help choosing wedding shoes?

   _____

4. Where should Paul shop for work shoes?

   _____

5. Where should Jeanne look at the latest shoe styles?

   _____

6. Where did Rolf look for golf shoes?

   _____

Unit D5: Dating

ask someone out (T-Sep): *to invite someone to do something or to go somewhere*

> She asked him out last weekend.
> I asked out your sister.

ask someone over (T-Sep) (OB): *to invite someone to one's house for a short visit*

> I asked him over.
> Who did he ask over?

break up (I): *to end a romantic relationship*

> Janet and Louis broke up yesterday.
> We broke up years ago.

call someone up (T-Sep): *to telephone someone*

> You called her up last night.
> I'll call up Lazlo.

fall for someone (T-Insep): *to fall in love with someone*

> Alicia fell for Phil.
> I fell for her the minute I saw her.

feel like something (T-Insep) informal: *to want to do or have something*

> I feel like taking a walk.
> Do you feel like pizza tonight?

go out (I): *to date or to go on a date*

> We've been going out for six months.
> Are you going out tonight?

go with someone (T-Insep): *to date someone steadily*

> I've been going with him for a year.
> She used to go with Brent.

make up (I): *to resolve a quarrel*

> Let's kiss and make up.
> The couple finally made up.

pick someone up (T-Sep): *to collect someone to go someplace*

> I'll pick you up at 8:00.
> He'll pick up his fiancée first.

Exercise 1

Fill in the blanks below with the correct verbs.

Example: Should I <u>ask</u> out your friend?

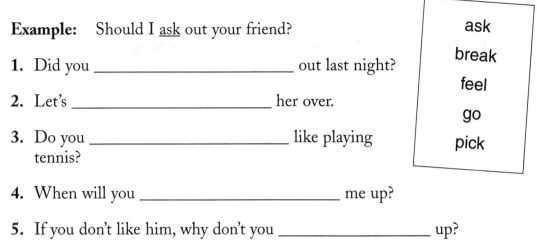

ask

break

feel

go

pick

1. Did you _____ out last night?

2. Let's _____ her over.

3. Do you _____ like playing tennis?

4. When will you _____ me up?

5. If you don't like him, why don't you _____ up?

Exercise 2

Circle the particle that correctly completes the sentence.

Example: How long have you been going _____ her?

      for   (with)   up

1. I'll call you _____ on the weekend.

      out   for   up

2. My brother really fell _____ her.

      for   up   like

3. Have they made _____ yet?

      with   over   up

4. Do you feel _____ having ice cream?

      like   up   out

5. My good friend asked my old roommate _____.

      out   with   up

Exercise 3

Rewrite the sentences to make them less formal, replacing the underlined part with a phrasal verb.

Example: We should <u>end our relationship.</u>
We should <u>break up.</u>

1. He'll <u>telephone</u> the girl this afternoon.

   _____

2. They are <u>going on a date</u> tonight.

   _____

3. Let's <u>resolve our quarrel.</u>

   _____

4. He <u>invited</u> his friend <u>to his house</u> to celebrate the end of his project.

   _____

5. She's been <u>dating</u> him for several years.

   _____

Exercise 4

Fill in the blanks below with the correct phrasal verbs.

Example: If you are not happy in your relationship, you should <u>break up</u>.

1. If you want her to see your stamp collection, you should

    _____ her _____.

2. If you want him to go to the show, just _____ him

    _____.

3. If you want to be with someone all the time, don't _____
    a traveling sales representative.

4. If you don't have a car, I'll _____ you

    _____.

5. If you want to talk to her, why don't you _____ her

    _____?

6. If you're not angry anymore, you should _____

    _____ .

Exercise 5a

Check the box next to the sentence that is written correctly.
Both sentences may be correct.

Example: ☒ He should call up Myra.
☒ He should call Myra up.

1. ☐ I feel like skiing today.
☐ I feel skiing like today.

2. ☐ Let's pick up your friend at 6:00.
☐ Let's pick your friend up at 6:00.

3. ☐ He's been going with her for years.
☐ He's been going her with for years.

4. ☐ Did you ask both couples over?
☐ Did you ask over both couples?

Exercise 5b

Use the words below to write complete sentences. Supply the correct
particles.

Example: she / Jaime / asked / last night
She asked Jaime out last night. *or* She asked out Jaime last
night.

1. feel / a cup of coffee / I / having

_____

2. Laura / him / went / for seven years

_____

3. can pick / he / at 7:00 / Karin

_____

4. fall / you / someone different / every month

_____

Exercise 6

Marco and Paul are making plans for Friday night. Read their conversation; then answer the questions about it in full sentences.

MARCO: Are you going to go out on Friday?

PAUL: Yeah. I'm going to ask Marta out.

MARCO: You really fell for her, didn't you? You just met her yesterday.

PAUL: Yeah. I know. There's something about her.

MARCO: Did you know she's going with Lars?

PAUL: She was going with Lars. She told me that they broke up.

MARCO: Lucky for you.

PAUL: Yeah. I know.

MARCO: Where are you going to go?

PAUL: I'm going to ask her over for dinner. Then I thought we'd go to the concert. Do you want to join us?

MARCO: Sure. Do you mind if I call up Min and invite her, too?

PAUL: No. Go ahead. Could you pick up both Min and Marta?

MARCO: Yeah. I'll pick them up at 6:00, okay?

PAUL: Yeah. Well, we'd better call them up first to see if they want to go.

Example: Who is Paul going to ask out?
<u>He's going to ask Marta out.</u>

1. Who did Paul fall for?

   _____

2. Who was Marta going with?

   _____

3. Who is asking Marta over for dinner?

   _____

4. Who is Marco going to call up?

   _____

5. What time is Marco going to pick up Min and Marta?

   _____

Unit D6: Travel

break down (I): *to stop functioning*
> The car broke down on the way to Yellowstone.
> Why did the train break down?

check in (I): *to register*
> We have to check in after 3:00.
> Let's check in before we go to dinner.

check out (I): *to settle one's bill before leaving a place that provides lodging*
> I checked out, so we can leave now.
> Have you checked out yet?

fuel/gas something up (T-Sep): *to fill something with fuel*
> Gas the car up before you go.
> They are fueling up the plane.

get back (I): *to return to where one lives*
> When did you get back?
> She got back last night.

get by (I): *to manage without something*
> I forgot my hair dryer, but I'll get by.
> How did you get by without your laptop?

pack something up (T-Sep): *to prepare something for transporting*
> Pack up your things! It's time to go.
> I packed everything up.

take off (I): *to depart*
> His plane takes off in ten minutes.
> When are you taking off for New York?

tire someone out (T-Sep): *to exhaust someone*
> Traveling tires me out.
> The hike tired out the kids.

wake up (I): *to awaken*
> We woke up early.
> He didn't wake up until 8:00.

Exercise 1

Fill in the blanks below with the correct verbs.

Example: Did your car <u>break</u> down on the freeway?

1. We don't have a lot of money, but we'll
   _____ by.

2. It's getting late. We should _____ in.

3. I forgot my alarm clock. How will I

   _____ up?

4. _____ up your suitcase.

5. I'll _____ back late, so don't wait for me.

> check
> get
> pack
> wake

Exercise 2

Circle the particle that correctly completes the sentence.

Example: What time did you wake _____?

    down   (up)   on

1. The plane is taking _____ right now.

       off   up   on

2. We need to gas _____ the car.

       out   in   up

3. What time did you check _____?

       out   up   on

4. Did the tour tire you _____?

       into   out   on

5. How long does it take to fuel the bus _____?

       into   on   up

Exercise 3

Rewrite the sentences to make them less formal, replacing the underlined part with a phrasal verb.

Example: Have you <u>registered</u> at the hotel yet?
<u>Have you checked in at the hotel yet?</u>

1. Did your rental car <u>stop functioning</u>?

    _____

2. I must <u>return home</u> early in the day.

    _____

3. We <u>managed</u> without a guide.

    _____

4. We <u>awoke</u> in a new place.

    _____

5. Should we <u>put gas into</u> the car?

    _____

Exercise 4

Fill in the blanks below with the correct phrasal verbs.

Example: They <u>fuel up</u> the plane as the passengers board.

1. Set your alarm so you _____ early.

2. When you need to stay in a new city, you must

    _____ at a hotel.

3. Your son is napping. Did the trip _____ him _____ ?

4. Don't worry. If you forget something, you'll _____.

5. We should _____ the car. The tank's almost empty.

Exercise 5

Fill in the blanks below with the correct particles.

Example: Where do we check <u>in</u>?

1. What time should we check _____?

2. What part of the trip tired you _____?

3. When did you get _____?

4. Without your glasses, how did you get _____?

5. When does the plane take _____?

Exercise 6

Choose a compound noun from the list. Change it to a verb phrase to complete the sentences below.

breakdown

check-in

takeoff

checkout

Example: A bus could <u>break down</u> in the left lane and block traffic.

1. The hotel manager said you must

   _____ by 11:00 A.M.

2. Their plane will _____ soon.

3. Why did the car have to _____ on a busy road?

4. The earliest we can _____ is 3:00 P.M.

Exercise 7

Ruben has written a postcard to his friend to thank him for his hospitality and to describe his hard trip home. Read the postcard; then answer the questions about it in full sentences.

January 15

Dear Leo,

Thank you for letting us stay with you. I enjoyed every minute of our visit, especially the trips to the beach. They were so relaxing. Our trip home, though, really tired me out. We had to rush in order to check in at the airport by 9:30. Vicky and I got back from the party so late the night before that I forgot to set the alarm clock. I didn't wake up until 7:30. Then we packed up our things so fast that I forgot my Walkman. (I'll get by somehow, but if you find it, will you send it to me?) At the airport, everything seemed to be going okay, but then they told us that something on the plane broke down and that we wouldn't take off until 2:00 in the afternoon. We finally got back to St. Paul at 10:00 p.m. Well, I should quit complaining because we had a great time with you. All that sunny weather was a good break from the cold here. Whenever I want to warm up, I'll think of you reading a book at the beach.

Take care,

Ruben

Example: What tired Ruben out?
<u>His trip home tired him out.</u>

1. What time was check-in at the airport?

_____

2. Why did Ruben forget to set the alarm?

_____

3. What time did Ruben wake up?

_____

4. Why did Ruben forget his Walkman?

_____

5. What happened to the plane?

_____

6. What time did the plane take off?

_____

Unit D7: Family

bring someone or something up (T-Sep): *to raise to adulthood*
> We brought up those children during a difficult time.
> They brought Fido up from a puppy.

get along (I): *to be amiable*
> Everyone in our family got along.
> Why didn't you get along?

grow into someone or something (T-Insep): *to become someone or something*
> The boy grew into an Olympic athlete.
> She grew into a fine person.

grow up (I): *to become an adult*
> All of our children have grown up.
> They grow up quickly.

hand something down (T-Sep): *to pass something on to a younger person or generation*
> The grandfather handed down his watch to his grandson.
> I will hand this down to my daughter.

hear from someone (T-Insep): *to receive a message from someone*
> She heard from an old friend yesterday.
> Have you heard from Clayton lately?

look after someone or something (T-Insep): *to take care of someone or something*
> He's looking after the children.
> Who's looking after the kittens?

pass away (I): *to die*
> My grandmother passed away last year.
> When did he pass away?

take after someone (T-Insep): *to resemble a relative*
> You take after your father.
> I take after her.

take something up (T-Sep): *to enter into a profession or to begin a hobby*
> Both of my sons took up architecture.
> My grandfather just took up golf.

Exercise 1

Fill in the blanks below with the correct verbs.

Example: Children <u>grow</u> up fast.

1. When do you think you'll _____ from your son?

2. You _____ after your uncle.

3. I'll _____ after the children today.

4. Do your sons _____ along?

5. What profession did your daughter

   _____ up?

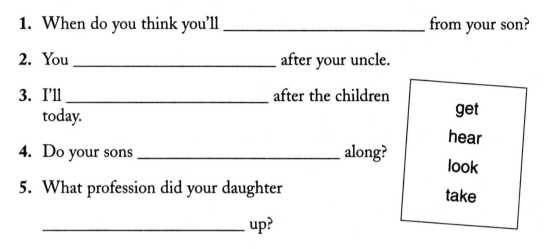

get

hear

look

take

Exercise 2

Circle the particle that correctly completes the sentence.

Example: My grandparents brought me _____.

   from   with   (up)

1. Her little boy grew _____ a man.

   into   for   up

2. She handed _____ her stamp collection to her niece.

   away   up   down

3. His great aunt passed _____ last month.

   from   away   up

4. I grew _____ in South Dakota.

   like   up   out

5. We haven't heard _____ our aunt in a long time.

   from   down   up

Exercise 3

Fill in the blanks with the correct phrasal verbs.

Example: I'm not going to raise those puppies; someone else will have to <u>bring</u> them <u>up</u>.

1. We never fight; we always _____.

2. My grandmother didn't _____; she's old, but she's still active.

3. I don't need this anymore; I'll _____ it _____ to my eldest daughter.

4. She can't watch the children today, but she can

   _____ them tomorrow.

5. Will you _____ your father's profession?

Exercise 4

Check the box next to the sentence that is written correctly. Both sentences may be correct.

Example: ☒ They brought up the child.
              ☒ They brought her up.

1. ☐ The spoiled child grew into a monster.
   ☐ The spoiled child grew it into.

2. ☐ He handed down a great legacy.
   ☐ He handed it down.

3. ☐ The parents heard from all of their children regularly.
   ☐ The parents heard them from regularly.

4. ☐ I'll look after the goldfish while you're away.
   ☐ I'll look them after while you're away.

5. ☐ They both take after Uncle Louie.
   ☐ They both take him after.

Exercise 5a

Fill in each relative clause below with the correct particles.

Example: The son who couldn't get <u>along</u> was the black sheep of the family.

1. The house where I grew _____ no longer exists.

2. The man who passed _____ was my cousin.

3. The profession he took _____ was very rewarding.

4. We sold the ponies we brought _____.

5. She grew _____ a person who was admired by everyone.

Exercise 5b

Use the words below to complete the sentences. Supply the correct particles.

Example: The furniture (*handed / she*) <u>she handed down</u> was from Norway.

1. The relative (*take / you / the most*) _____ is your great-grandfather.

2. The children (*every day / look / I*) _____ are my sister's.

3. The town (*where / he / grew*) _____ was very small.

4. The daughter (*I / yesterday / heard*) _____ lives in Mexico City.

5. I never met the uncle (*take / I*) _____.

Exercise 6

Susan has written a letter to her good friend Linda. Read her letter; then answer the questions about it in full sentences.

> Dear Linda,
>
> I am sorry I haven't written in such a long time. The twins, Alec and Andrew, have been keeping me busy. They are growing up fast, though, and becoming quite independent. I can't believe they are already nine years old.
>
> I'm surprised by what interesting kids they've turned into. They seem interesting to me because they don't take after either Jack or me. Alec is fascinated by fossils. Andrew likes to go fossil hunting, too, but he's more interested in weather prediction. Jack thinks Andrew will take up meteorology as a career someday. Even though the boys have different interests, they get along.
>
> I have some sad news to tell you. After fighting cancer for five years, Greg passed away. His funeral is on Saturday. Jack said that he would look after the boys so I can attend it. I'll say some prayers for you. We had fun together, didn't we?
>
> Linda, I know you're busy, too, but if you have a few minutes, write. I'd love to hear from you.
>
> Love,
> Susan

Example: What has happened to Linda's kids as they have grown up?
<u>Her kids have become independent as they have grown up.</u>

1. Do the kids take after Susan or Jack?

   _____

2. Has Linda heard from Susan recently?

   _____

3. What career might Andrew take up?

   _____

4. Who passed away?

   _____

5. What is Susan surprised by?

   _____

6. Who would Susan like to hear from?

   _____

Unit D8: Weather

call something off (T-Sep): *to cancel something*
>We called off the game because of the rain.
>Should we call the family picnic off?

clear up (I): *to become clear*
>It has cleared up. Let's go outside.
>The sky is clearing up.

cloud up (I): *to become cloudy*
>It's clouding up.
>The sky clouded up.

cool off (I): *to become cool*
>After the sun set, it cooled off.
>I cooled off in the swimming pool.

dry off (I): *to become dry*
>It was wet this morning, but this afternoon, it dried off.
>Dry off with a towel.

let up (I): *to subside*
>The rain is letting up.
>We will be able to see when the snow lets up.

put something on (T-Sep): *to dress in a piece of clothing*
>Put on your coat! It's cold outside.
>I put a hat on.

set in (I): *to become fixed*
>Cold weather has set in.
>Low pressure set in yesterday.

take something off (T-Sep): *to remove a piece of clothing*
>When the sun came out, I took off my jacket.
>Take your shoes off when you enter their house.

warm up (I): *to become warm*
>The day is really warming up.
>Warm up by the fire.

Exercise 1

Fill in the blanks below with the correct verbs.

Example: Did they <u>call</u> off the soccer match?

1. It's hot now, but it should _____ off tonight.

2. The rain _____ up, and
    the sun came out.

3. It's very sunny out, so you should

    _____ on a sun hat.

4. Good weather _____ in.
    I hope it stays.

5. It's cold out. Go inside and _____ up.

cool
let
put
set
warm

Exercise 2

Circle the particle that correctly completes the sentence.

Example: The sky should clear _____ today.

   in   (up)   on

1. I dried _____ by sitting in the sun.

   in   off   on

2. The sky clouded _____ this afternoon.

   on   off   up

3. I took _____ my gloves, so I could write a note.

   off   on   up

4. They called school _____ because of the snow.

   in   on   off

5. Let's cool _____ with a cold glass of lemonade.

   off   on   in

Exercise 3a

Write a response to the statements below. Use the form "Why don't you ...?" Choose a verb from the first column and a noun phrase from the second column. Supply the correct particles.

```
call        your raincoat
put         a wide-brimmed hat
take        the meeting
            your sweater
            the game
            your sunglasses
```

Example: It's hot in here.
<u>Why don't you take off your sweater?</u>

1. I'm going to get a sunburn on my face.

   _____

2. The baseball players won't be able to see the ball in this fog.

   _____

3. I'm getting wet.

   _____

4. Committee members shouldn't drive on these slippery roads.

   _____

5. It's gotten dark out.

   _____

Exercise 3b

Now write responses to the statements below. Use pronouns instead of noun phrases.

Example: This sweater is too hot.
Why don't you take it off?

1. I brought this wide-brimmed hat with me.

   _____

2. It's too foggy for the game.

   _____

3. I have a raincoat with me.

   _____

4. The meeting isn't very important.

   _____

5. These sunglasses make everything look very dark.

   _____

Exercise 3c

What happens to the phrasal verbs above when you use pronoun objects?

_____

Exercise 4

Complete the complaints below using the form "When is it going to ...?"
Choose a verb from the list. Supply the correct particles.

Example: My flowers need rain.
<u>When is it going to cloud up?</u>

1. It's too muddy to go for a walk.

    _____

2. It's been raining hard for hours.

    _____

3. It has been a cold spring.

    _____

4. I'll die in this heat.

    _____

5. It has been cloudy since Monday.

    _____

clear
cloud
cool
dry
let
warm

Exercise 5

Read the transcript of "Wally's Weather Talk" below; then answer the questions in complete sentences.

> Hi. I'm Wally Worthington. Welcome to Weather Talk. Let's see, here in Elgin, it clouded up yesterday evening and started to rain around midnight. Well, the rain should let up by tomorrow morning. A high-pressure system will set in, so it will clear up and dry off, but it will probably cool off a bit too. If you're going to be out tomorrow, you may want to put on a sweater. By Sunday, though, it will warm up again, so if you're still wearing the sweater, you may want to take it off.

Example: When did it cloud up in Elgin?
<u>It clouded up yesterday.</u>

1. Should people put on light jackets or raincoats today?

   _____

2. When will the rain let up?

   _____

3. What type of pressure system will set in?

   _____

4. What will happen when the high-pressure system sets in?

   _____

5. What type of clothing should we put on tomorrow?

   _____

6. What will the weather do on Sunday?

   _____

Unit D9: Entertaining

clear something away (T-Sep): *to remove something*
Please clear the dishes away.
We cleared away the snow in front of the door.

cook/mix/stir something up (T-Sep): *to prepare a type of food or drink*
She cooked up a delicious dinner.
I'll mix the cookie dough up.

dish/serve something up (T-Sep): *to serve something*
He's dishing up the lasagna.
When are you serving up dinner?

drink something up, eat something up (T-Sep): *to drink or eat all of something*
They ate up all the appetizers.
Did you drink the punch up?

get to something (T-Insep): *to attend to something*
I didn't get to the invitations today.
We got to our chores in the afternoon.

go over (I): *to be received*
How did the party go over?
It didn't go over very well.

have someone over (T-Sep) (OB): *to invite someone to one's house for a short visit*
Let's have the neighbors over tonight.
They had us over for dinner.

look something up (T-Sep): *to seek something*
I must look up the recipe.
Look it up in the phone book.

pick something out (T-Sep): *to choose something*
I picked out some good cheese for our party.
Did you pick out the music yet?

see someone off (T-Sep): *to accompany someone as he or she is leaving*
Corrie, will you see off our guests?
You don't have to see me off.

Exercise 1

Fill in the blanks below with the correct verbs.

Example: He'll <u>cook</u> up something from his country.

1. Are you leaving? I'll _____ you off.

2. _____ out your favorite flavor of ice cream for dessert.

3. You should _____ up his address in the company directory.

4. I didn't _____ to my homework, because I went to the party.

5. How did the dinner _____ over?

get

go

look

pick

see

Exercise 2

Circle the particle that correctly completes the sentence.

Example: Should I mix _____ some drinks?

     away   out   (up)

1. Clear that _____. I need some room.

     on   away   in

2. The children ate _____ all the rolls.

     over   up   out

3. Let's have guests _____.

     to   over   off

4. Dinner's ready, so we should dish it _____.

     off   up   away

5. Have you picked _____ something to wear?

     off   out   up

Exercise 3

Read the request; then put a check next to the correctly written sentence.

Example: Should I dish up the dessert?
        ☒ Yes, dish it up.
        ☐ Yes, dish up it.

1. Should I stir up the sauce?
   ☐ Yes, stir up it.
   ☐ Yes, stir it up.

2. Should I clear away the dishes?
   ☐ Yes, clear them away.
   ☐ Yes, clear away them.

3. Should we pick out some snacks for the kids while we're at the store?
   ☐ Yes, let's let Lucy pick them out.
   ☐ Yes, let's let Lucy pick out them.

4. Should we have the Abdalas over?
   ☐ Yes, let's have over them.
   ☐ Yes, let's have them over.

5. Should I serve up the red beans and rice now?
   ☐ No, serve them up in about ten minutes.
   ☐ No, serve up them in about ten minutes.

Exercise 4

Fill in the blanks below with the correct particles.

Example: What kind of music did you pick <u>out</u>?

1. Who are you seeing _____?

2. What didn't you get _____?

3. What are you cooking _____?

4. Who should we have _____?

5. What should I look _____?

Exercise 5

Rewrite the passive-voice sentence as a sentence in the active voice. Use he or she as the subject.

Example: Our meal was served up.
              <u>He served up our meal.</u> *or* <u>He served our meal up.</u>

1. The decorations were picked out two weeks before the party.

   _____

2. The salad was dished up.

   _____

3. The dishes were cleared away.

   _____

4. Everything was eaten up.

   _____

5. The pasta was cooked up in ten minutes.

   _____

Exercise 6

Use a noun phrase from the first column and a verb phrase from the second column to create a sentence in the passive voice. Supply the appropriate particle.

the cake batter	were eaten
all the cocoa	were seen
the ripest tomatoes	was cleared
the mess	were picked
the guests	was stirred
all the rolls	was drunk

Example: All the cocoa was drunk up.

1. _____

2. _____

3. _____

4. _____

5. _____

Exercise 7

Alberto and Binh are catering a big party. They have been preparing for it all day. Even though they have divided up the tasks, they are not finished. Read their checklist; then answer the questions below in complete sentences.

☒ pick out some small candles for the tables (Alberto)
☒ clear away chairs from the dance floor (Binh)
☒ look up the recipes (Alberto)
☐ stir up the soup (Binh)
☒ mix up the ingredients for the spring rolls (Alberto)
☐ cook up the potatoes (Binh)
☐ serve up the appetizers (Binh)
☐ dish up the dessert (Alberto)

Example: Has Binh cleared away the chairs?
<u>Yes, Binh has cleared them away.</u>

1. What did Alberto look up?

_____

2. What did Alberto mix up ingredients for?

_____

3. What should Binh do to the soup so the ingredients are well blended?

_____

4. What should Binh cook up?

_____

5. Did Alberto pick out flowers or candles for the table decorations?

_____

6. Who should serve up the appetizers, and who should dish up the dessert?

_____

Unit D10: Business

add something up (T-Sep): *to total a set of numbers*
Add up the costs.
The accountant added them up.

bail someone or something out (T-Sep): *to help someone or something in difficulty*
If I get in trouble, will you bail me out?
The government had to bail out some financial institutions.

buy something up (T-Sep): *to buy all of something*
They bought up the entire supply.
We bought them up.

fall through (I): *to fail*
Our plans fell through.
Why did the deal fall through?

figure something in (T-Sep): *to include something*
I figured in the costs for housing.
We should figure that in, too.

lay someone off (T-Sep): *to end someone's employment*
The company laid off 30 employees.
They laid them off two weeks ago.

open something up (T-Sep): *to start a business or to begin business for the day*
We opened a new shop up in Rochester.
What time do you open up your shop?

pay something off (T-Sep): *to pay the total amount*
Have you paid off your loan?
I will pay it off next month.

sell something off (T-Sep): *to sell, usually at a low or reduced price*
We sold off the old office furniture.
You should sell off your extra supply.

shut something down (T-Sep): *to stop operating*
The owner shut down his business.
She shut it down a year ago.

Exercise 1

Fill in the blanks below with the correct verbs.

Example: Someone should <u>open</u> up a bakery in this town.

buy

fall

pay

sell

shut

1. He's dependable, so your agreement shouldn't

_____ through.

2. I _____ off my bills.

3. The business wasn't making money, so they _____ it down.

4. Let's _____ up all the stock before the price
goes up.

5. They must _____ off the entire inventory.

Exercise 2

Circle the particle that correctly completes the sentence.

Example: Did you add _____ our profits for the year?

in   through   (up)

1. I didn't figure _____ a raise for next year's budget.

in   off   down

2. They will lay _____ fifteen employees next week.

off   up   down

3. My older brother bailed me _____.

through   out   up

4. I opened _____ the office early yesterday.

down   up   in

5. Our offer fell _____.

off   through   down

Exercise 3

Fill in the blanks below with the correct particles.

Example: What fell <u>through</u>?

1. How many people did they lay _____?

2. How many businesses did he buy _____?

3. When was the theater shut _____?

4. Where will the new business open _____?

5. Which column of numbers did you add _____?

6. How many of the extra expenses did you figure _____?

▌Exercise 4

Choose a compound noun from the list; then change it to a verb phrase to complete the sentences below.

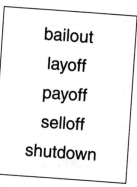

bailout

layoff

payoff

selloff

shutdown

Example: The company needed to <u>lay off</u> a thousand workers.

1. Do you think the government should _____ corporations that run out of money?

2. GWM Industries wanted to _____ seventy employees.

3. We are going to _____ those loans by the end of the year.

4. The government ordered the plant to _____ because it was not safe.

5. They will _____ the inventory and use the profit to buy new machinery.

Exercise 5

Change the active sentence to a sentence in the passive voice. Omit the by phrase.

Example: She added up the charges.
<u>The charges were added up.</u>

1. He didn't figure in the cost of the equipment.

   _____

2. I didn't open up the restaurant until 5:00.

   _____

3. We bailed them out.

   _____

4. We finally sold off our old office building.

   _____

5. The owner shut down the plant in Kansas.

   _____

Exercise 6

Use the object in the first sentence as the subject in the second sentence. The verb phrase will become intransitive. This transformation can only occur with the verbs presented.

Example: She opened up a new pet store in town.
<u>A new pet store opened up in town.</u>

1. They shut down the factory in Pasco.

   _____

2. He opened up the gas station every day at 6:00.

   _____

Exercise 7

T. J. Owner had a bad year. His office supply business is not doing well, so he has made a list of actions he needs to take in order to avoid bankruptcy. Read through his list; then answer the questions about it in full sentences.

- review reasons some transactions fell through
- shut down out-of-state stores
- sell off inventory from out-of-state stores
- pay off loans
- lay off a hundred employees at in-state stores
- buy up manufacturers' low-priced items
- open up copy centers in existing stores

Example: What will T. J. Owner review?
<u>He will review the reasons some transactions fell through.</u>

1. Which stores will T. J. Owner shut down?

   _____

2. Which stores will open up copy centers?

   _____

3. What will T. J. Owner buy up?

   _____

4. What does T. J. Owner think he should pay off?

   _____

5. Who will be laid off?

   _____

6. What will T. J. Owner do with the inventory from out-of-state stores?

   _____

Unit DII: Discussion

bring something up (T-Sep): *to mention something*
> Someone should bring up the topic.
> You should bring it up.

cut in (I): *to interrupt*
> Tom always cuts in when I speak.
> Don't cut in during my presentation!

hear someone out (T-Sep) (OB): *to hear all of what someone says*
> Please, hear me out!
> I've heard you out.

quiet down (I): *to become quiet*
> The class finally quieted down.
> Quiet down so we can hear him.

shout someone down (T-Sep): *to stop someone from speaking by shouting*
> They shouted down the politician.
> He shouted you down.

shut up (I) rude: *to stop speaking*
> She shut up when I walked in the room.
> I'll shut up; I've talked long enough.

speak out (I): *to speak freely*
> If you care about it, speak out.
> Speak out and let people know what's on your mind!

speak up (I): *to speak louder*
> The lecturer spoke up so everyone could hear.
> Speak up, please.

talk around something (T-Insep): *to speak indirectly about something*
> He just talks around the problem.
> Don't talk around the issue. Get to the point!

talk something over (T-Sep): *to discuss something*
> We should talk over this matter in private.
> May I talk this over with you?

Exercise 1

Fill in the blanks below with the correct verbs.

Example: Did the student <u>shout</u> down the professor?

1. Let's _____ him out. He may have something interesting to say.

2. Someone should _____ up that issue at our next meeting.

3. _____ down! I can't hear.

4. You just _____ around the topic.

5. Why do you always _____ in when I'm talking?

bring

cut

quiet

hear

talk

Exercise 2

Circle the particle that correctly completes the sentence.

Example: He brought _____ a good point.

   in   over   (up)

1. When the topic of injustice comes up, he'll speak _____.

   in   over   out

2. Does he ever shut _____?

   in   up   out

3. No one can hear them. They should speak _____.

   down   over   up

4. Why do you talk _____ the topic instead of getting to the point?

   over   up   around

5. Let's talk _____ your role in the meeting.

   out   over   up

Exercise 3

Rewrite the sentences to make them less formal, replacing the underlined part with a phrasal verb.

Example: Don't <u>interrupt</u>.
              <u>Don't cut in.</u>

1. The gossip <u>stopped speaking</u> immediately when a friend came into the room.

   _____

2. Could you <u>speak louder</u>?

   _____

3. The owner <u>stopped</u> the union representative <u>from speaking by shouting</u>.

   _____

4. The children finally <u>became quiet</u>.

   _____

5. Let's <u>discuss</u> the matter.

   _____

Exercise 4

Complete the sentences with phrasal verbs in their infinitive forms.

Example: If you want her to mention something at the meeting, ask her
<u>to bring it up.</u>

1. If you want them to listen to all of what you have to say, ask them

    _____.

2. If you can't hear him, you should ask him _____.

3. If you don't like their interruptions, ask them not _____.

4. If he has something important to say, tell him _____.

Exercise 5

Rewrite the sentences below. Change the underlined noun phrase to
a pronoun.

Example: Did you bring up <u>the subject</u>?
<u>Did you bring it up?</u>

1. Ernie shouted down <u>his opponents</u>.

    _____

2. We'll hear <u>the students</u> out.

    _____

3. He talks around <u>any controversial topic</u>.

    _____

4. We talked over <u>the event</u>.

    _____

5. Did anyone bring up <u>her record</u>?

    _____

Exercise 6

You attended a meeting at which you knew no one except your friend. After the meeting, you ask her about the other participants. Use the expression "Who was the person who . . . ?"

Example: You noticed that someone always cut in while others were speaking.
<u>Who was the person who always cut in while others were speaking?</u>

1. You noticed that someone brought up personal topics.

   _____

2. You were surprised that someone never spoke up.

   _____

3. You noticed that someone talked around the topic of library funding.

   _____

4. You were angry that someone never shut up for very long.

   _____

5. You were upset that someone didn't hear you out.

   _____

Exercise 7

The following is a transcript from a city advisory commission meeting.
Read it; then answer the questions about it in complete sentences.

> ALICE: I would like to talk about our local pollution problem today.
>
> SIMON: I would, too. As you know, I have argued fervently against allowing . . .
>
> ANTON: Wait a minute. I think we need to discuss funding for the town soccer team first. The season starts in two weeks, and the team still doesn't have uniforms.
>
> RITA: (something spoken softly)
>
> ANTON: I'm sorry. I didn't hear you.
>
> RITA: I think we should listen to what Simon has to say. So far the City Council has only talked around the issue of pollution control. We need to come up with a proposal by Thursday night.

Example: What topic has the City Council been talking around?
<u>The City Council has been talking around the issue of pollution control.</u>

1. Who brought up the topic of local pollution?

   _____

2. Who has spoken out in the past on that topic?

   _____

3. Who cut in?

   _____

4. Who was not heard out?

   _____

5. Who was asked to speak up?

   _____

6. What did Rita want to talk over?

   _____

Unit D12: Training

brush up on something (Insep): *to refresh one's knowledge of something*
> I should brush up on my French before I leave for Montreal.
> He brushed up on the subject.

come up to something (Insep): *to meet or fulfill something*
> Does Marco's work come up to our standards?
> Her performance didn't come up to our expectations.

come up with something (Insep): *to find or generate something*
> She came up with a great idea.
> I couldn't come up with the answer.

fill in for someone or something (Insep): *to substitute for someone or something*
> I will be gone, so Harmon will fill in for me.
> What can fill in for my missed assignment?

get along with someone (Insep): *to be friendly with someone*
> The trainees all get along with one another.
> Kim gets along with no one.

get out of something: (Insep): *to free oneself of a responsibility*
> I got out of that difficult assignment.
> Did you get out of writing the paper?

keep up with something (Insep): *to remain knowledgeable about current events or current thought*
> Do you keep up with current events?
> I keep up with new theories.

look forward to something (Insep): *to anticipate something eagerly*
> We look forward to your lecture.
> I'm not looking forward to the test.

read up on someone or something (Insep): *to study about someone or something by reading*
> Read up on Bacon so you understand his ideas.
> I read up on the Industrial Revolution.

study up on someone or something (Insep): *to study thoroughly*
> We studied up on Eleanor Roosevelt for our presentation.
> You should study up on the civil rights movement.

Exercise 1

Fill in the blanks below with the correct verbs.

Example: Did you <u>brush</u> up on your algebra?

1. Who should _____ in for the teacher when she is absent?

2. I _____ forward to my new job.

3. You can't _____ out of that commitment.

4. She must _____ up with current thought.

5. Did you _____ up with a plan?

> come
>
> fill
>
> get
>
> keep
>
> look

Exercise 2

Circle the particle that correctly completes the sentence.

Example: Her work didn't come _____ to our standard of excellence.

    (up)   along   to

1. I should study _____ on verb conjugation before I take the language test.

        in   up   with

2. They get _____ with everyone.

        about   along   for

3. The medical student brushed _____ on anatomy before taking his exam.

        in   for   up

4. He gets _____ of doing his work by lying.

        out   for   along

5. Can you fill _____ for me tomorrow?

        in   to   over

Exercise 3

Fill in the blanks below with the correct particles and prepositions.

Example: Have you kept <u>up with</u> the new findings?

1. She must come _____ a proposal by tomorrow.

2. I look _____ working with you.

3. He studied _____ the recent improvements in computer printers.

4. To work here, you must get _____ the manager.

5. I'll fill _____ you while you're away.

Exercise 4a

Check the box next to the sentence that is written correctly.

Example: ☒ They got out of their responsibilities.
           ☐ They got of their responsibilities out.

1. ☐ A retired manager filled for our trainer in.
   ☐ A retired manager filled in for our trainer.

2. ☐ I haven't kept up with the recent changes.
   ☐ I haven't kept with the recent changes up.

3. ☐ She brushed up on nutrition for her nursing exam.
   ☐ She brushed on nutrition up for her nursing exam.

4. ☐ They came with an astonishing design up.
   ☐ They came up with an astonishing design.

5. ☐ The students looked forward to finishing their program.
   ☐ The students looked to finishing their program forward.

Exercise 4b

Where does the particle always occur in phrasal-prepositional verbs?

_____

Exercise 5

You are working with a team. Use the expression "Let's ..." to suggest group action.

Example: <u>Let's brush up on</u> our Spanish so we can communicate with the workers at the Mexican plant.

1. _____ a design that will impress our supervisor.

2. _____ the policy in the office manual.

3. _____ new knowledge by studying all current reports.

4. _____ one another when we have to be gone.

5. _____ the latest model so we can improve it.

Exercise 6

Change these sentences into questions. The wh- word replaces the underlined words. Remember to change first-person pronouns to second-person pronouns.

Example: They're studying up on <u>a new computer language</u>.
What <u>are they studying up on?</u>

1. He gets along with <u>the other workers</u>.

   Who _____?

2. I got out of <u>working on Saturdays</u>.

   What _____?

3. We're looking forward to <u>a vacation</u>.

   What _____?

4. She's reading up on <u>the company's history</u>.

   What _____?

5. They came up with <u>some interesting data</u>.

   What _____?

Exercise 7

Your friend Marnie is having problems in her training program. Her supervisor and the other trainees have made the following complaints about her. Read over the complaints; then write down advice for Marnie that will help her succeed in her program. Begin your advice with "You should/shouldn't . . ."

> Marnie doesn't get along with anybody.
>
> Marnie doesn't keep up with current thought in our field.
>
> Marnie doesn't come up with any original ideas.
>
> Marnie always asks other people to fill in for her.
>
> Marnie doesn't study up on necessary research.
>
> Marnie always gets out of doing her share of the work.
>
> Marnie doesn't read up on important procedures.

Example: <u>You should get along with everybody.</u>

1. _____

2. _____

3. _____

4. _____

5. _____

6. _____

Answers

Adjective Phrases

These are suggested answers. In some cases, other answers are possible.

Unit A1: Enchantment
Exercise 1a
1. enchanted
2. captivated
3. amazed
4. amused
5. beguiled
6. bewitched
7. charmed

Exercise 1b
by

Exercise 2a
1. amazed by their success
2. captivated by the soundtrack
3. bewitched by his soft voice
4. fascinated by Martin's athletic ability
5. entranced by the color of the sunset
6. charmed by the young boy
7. beguiled by my friend's sister

Exercise 2b
When participles refer to emotions, the preposition *by* is commonly used. Many grammars refer to this construction as the passive voice.

Exercise 3a
1. enthralled by the symphony's performance of Beethoven's Fifth
2. amused by the book
3. beguiled by her smile
4. amazed by the band
5. charmed by our guide
6. enchanted by the small cottage
7. fascinated by his paintings

Exercise 3b
The past participle (*-ed* form) is used to refer to the experiencer. <u>He</u> was enchanted by the song.

The present participle (*-ing* form) is used to refer to the cause of the experience. <u>The song</u> was enchanting.

Exercise 4
1. Was the audience captivated by the speech?
2. Were the young musicians enthralled by Segovia?
3. Were you entranced by his personality?
4. Were you fascinated by the novel?
5. Weren't you amazed by his memory?
6. Weren't you amused by her conversation?
7. Weren't the guests charmed by the welcome gift?
8. Weren't you enchanted by the entire evening?

Exercise 5
1. They are charmed by Gene.
2. She is beguiled by Gene's music.
3. The audience is captivated by Gene's solo performance.
4. They are both amused by the playfulness of the otters at the zoo.
5. He is fascinated by both Jenny and Julie.

6. They will be bewitched by the way three loose strings are pulled together.

Unit A2: Satisfaction
Exercise 1
1. satisfied
2. uneasy
3. disappointed
4. comfortable
5. discontented

Exercise 2
1. with
2. with
3. about
4. with
5. with

Exercise 3
1. We're unhappy about the rejection.
2. We're content with a week of vacation.
3. We were delighted with the award.
4. We were disappointed in his sloppy work.
5. We were pleased with the good news.
6. We were displeased with his thoughtless actions.
7. We were satisfied with a simple life.
8. We were dissatisfied with low overtime pay.

Exercise 4a
1. disappointed in my work
2. uneasy about the project
3. displeased with the new camera
4. satisfied with their new toys
5. happy about my promotion

6. dissatisfied with the company's service
7. delighted with his new kite

Exercise 4b
Usually, a preposition that follows a noun will also be used after the corresponding adjective. *Delighted* differs from the others because it is followed by *with* while the noun *delight* is followed by *in*.

Exercise 5
1. with
   He is comfortable with James Marshik.
2. with
   She is dissatisfied with the microwave oven.
3. about
   She was uneasy about answering the interviewer's question.
4. with
   I was most content with my work as a sports writer.
5. with
   They are displeased with Room 4A.
6. about
   She is unhappy about her heavy workload.

Exercise 6
1. She was dissatisfied with the fish.
2. She was delighted with the Bach cantatas.
3. She was disappointed in the wall decorations.
4. She was pleased with the lilies.
5. Yes, she was content with the coffee service.
6. She was displeased with the waitress serving the champagne.

Unit A3: Work
Exercise 1
1. prepared
2. absent
3. competent
4. dedicated
5. impressed

Exercise 2
1. for
2. at
3. about
4. to
5. to

Exercise 3
1. competent in international relations
2. dedicated to helping the homeless
3. present at every conference
4. necessary for this job
5. prepared for the closure of the plant
6. unqualified for the position
7. enthusiastic about our plan
8. absent from work

Exercise 4
1. with
   The manager was most impressed with Mr. Hebert.
2. from
   She was absent from the two morning sessions.
3. in
   They are competent in botany and math.
4. to
   They are dedicated to their families.
5. for
   It is necessary for repairing the office machines.
6. with
   She was unimpressed with the candidate's previous experience.

Exercise 5
1. No, recommendations are not necessary for all jobs.
2. No, someone without experience would not be qualified for the job as electrician.
3. No, the manager would be unimpressed with an applicant who has no experience as an electrician.
4. They must be prepared for heavy work.
5. No training is necessary for the position of groundskeeper.

Unit A4: Connections
Exercise 1
1. dependent
2. relevant
3. connected
4. independent
5. tied

Exercise 2
1. upon
2. to
3. to
4. to
5. to

Exercise 3a
1. Economics is connected to ethics.
2. Field hockey is similar to ice hockey.
3. Sanskrit is related to Latin.
4. His novel is not comparable to John Updike's.
5. A nectarine is similar to a peach.

Exercise 3b
No, *akin* must always be followed by *to*.

Exercise 4
1. upon
2. on
3. of
4. to
5. to

Exercise 5
1. tied to his family
2. connected to the incident
3. related to smoking
4. irrelevant to the case
5. dependent on drugs
6. similar to classical music
7. comparable to the sound of a flute

Exercise 6
1. He says football players are comparable to nurses.
2. He says the popularity of sports was contingent upon the invention of the automobile.
3. He says that baseball is similar to volleyball.
4. He says that riding a bike is akin to hitting a golf ball.
5. He says that amateurs are dependent on their shoes for success.
6. He says failure is tied to practicing too much.

Unit A5: Turmoil
Exercise 1
1. envious
2. angry
3. tired
4. disgusted
5. mad

Exercise 2
1. about
2. with
3. of
4. with
5. with

Exercise 3
1. furious with their incompetence

2. envious of his teammates
3. jealous of his fellow musicians
4. angry about the accident
5. disgusted with the incident

Exercise 4
1. at
2. about
3. of
4. with
5. with

Exercise 5
1. about
   Who was the person who was angry about the tuition hike?
2. with
   Who was the person who was disgusted with the cut in the library budget?
3. with
   Who was the person who was fed up with the poor athletics programs?
4. with
   Who was the person who was furious with the Dean of Student Affairs?
5. of
   Who was the person who was tired of receiving so little financial aid?
6. of
   Who was the person who was sick of the cafeteria food?

Exercise 6
1. They will be envious of citizens from Shoreview and Rosemont.
2. She is furious with the city council's decision to sell off East Lake Park to developers.
3. Ella does not get mad at others easily.
4. She is extremely angry at the city council.
5. She is fed up with the council members' arrogance.

6. All citizens of Lake City who are tired of hasty council decisions should write to the council members.

Unit A6: Attraction
Exercise 1
1. devoted
2. fond
3. engaged
4. infatuated
5. married

Exercise 2
1. with
2. of
3. to
4. to
5. of

Exercise 3
1. to
   I don't know who she is married to.
2. to
   I don't know who they are close to.
3. to
   I don't know what project he is devoted to.
4. to
   I don't know who she is engaged to.
5. with
   I don't know what kinds of ideas she is taken with.
6. of
   I don't know what kind of coffee-break treats they are fond of.

Exercise 4
1. John isn't fond of ice cream.
2. Atsuko is not engaged to James.
3. Lee is married to Julia.
4. Clara is devoted to the equal rights movement.
5. She is very attached to her high school friends.

6. Even though she was good looking, he wasn't attracted to her.
7. My aunt is enamored of roses.
8. Arnie is quite taken with this place.

Exercise 5
1. She was engaged to someone when she was eighteen.
2. She would like to be close to someone who likes to travel.
3. No, she is not attracted to someone who likes to watch TV. She is attracted to someone who is interested in foreign languages and cultures.
4. She is devoted to her job as a mapmaker.
5. No, she is not fond of hamburgers and french fries. She is fond of all types of ethnic food.
6. She was quite taken with *Dances with Wolves* and *Black Robe*.

Unit A7: School
Exercise 1
1. bored
2. engaged
3. unaccustomed
4. proud
5. responsible

Exercise 2
1. of
2. of
3. of
4. to
5. to

Exercise 3
1. Most children are accustomed to sharing lockers.
2. Students are open to learning new things.

3. Students are proud of getting good grades.
4. Students are responsible for leading discussions.
5. Students are used to helping others.
6. The librarian was unaware of disturbing the students.
7. Some preschoolers are incapable of sitting still.
8. By second grade, students are capable of listening to long stories.

Exercise 4
1. with
Who was the person who was bored with the history lecture?
2. of
Who was the person who was incapable of being quiet during class?
3. in
Who was the person who was engaged in a loud conversation with the biology professor?
4. for
Who was the person who was responsible for giving new students a campus tour?
5. of
Who was the person who was unaware of the registration deadline?
6. to
Who was the person who was used to living in dormitories?

Exercise 5
1. Anyone bored with college life should hike up the Ridge Trail with the Outing Club.
2. Anyone incapable of running a mile should get in shape with the Outing Club.

3. A student who is open to adventure should camp with the Outing Club at the summit of Mt. Hart.
4. They are used to walking, biking, and skiing long distances.
5. Students unaware of all the fun they could have should call Jason to find out more about the Outing Club.
6. They are proud of having fun.

Unit A8: Talent
Exercise 1
1. talented
2. blessed
3. confident
4. expert
5. unrivaled

Exercise 2
1. with
2. of
3. at
4. at
5. with

Exercise 3a
1. Carlo is talented at writing catchy tunes.
2. Carlo is good at entertaining all types of people.
3. Carlo is sure of getting lots of laughs.
4. Carlo is confident of being able to make people happy.

Exercise 3b
1. Carlo was so talented at writing catchy tunes that he was hired immediately.
2. Carlo was so good at entertaining all types of people that he was hired immediately.

3. Carlo was so sure of getting lots of laughs that he was hired immediately.
4. Carlo was so confident of being able to make people happy that he was hired immediately.

Exercise 4a
1. Isn't Lin expert at anything?
2. Isn't Lin good at anything?
3. Wasn't Lin gifted with anything?
4. Wasn't Lin blessed with anything?
5. Isn't Lin confident of anything?

Exercise 4b
1. What is Lin expert at?
2. What is Lin good at?
3. What was Lin gifted with?
4. What was Lin blessed with?
5. What is Lin confident of?

Exercise 5
1. She is sure of victory over the Waves.
2. They have been unrivaled in spiking talent.
3. Mary Andrews is expert at setting up spiking opportunities.
4. Yes, there are players besides Andrews who are good at setting.
5. No, without Andrews, the team wouldn't be confident of winning.
6. She is sure of her ability to perform.

Unit A9: Kindness
Exercise 1
1. grateful
2. sorry

3. thoughtful
4. sensitive
5. thankful

Exercise 2
1. of
2. to
3. for
4. of
5. of

Exercise 3
Answers may vary. Here are some possible answers.
1. It was nice of you to invite me to dinner.
2. It was kind of you to help me with my work.
3. It was thoughtful of you to send me flowers when I was sick.
4. It was good of you to take Grandma to the clinic.
5. It was kind of you to allow me to have an extra day of vacation.
6. It was nice of you to take care of my cat while I was away.
7. It was good of you to clean Mr. Fowler's house for him.
8. It was thoughtful of you to water my plants for me while I was away.

Exercise 4
1. What were they indebted to the staff for?
2. What was she sorry for?
3. What were the farmers thankful for?
4. What is Ms. Brady sensitive to?
5. What was the patient appreciative of?
6. What was it nice of him to do?
7. What was it good of Grandpa to do?
8. What was it thoughtful of the teacher to do?

Exercise 5
1. Roberto is thankful for Sara's organizational skills.
2. The staff is indebted to Sara for their success.
3. Stefan is grateful for Sara's work on projects.
4. Jerry is appreciative of Sara's thoughtfulness.
5. Samantha thinks it's kind of Sara to give their clients special attention.
6. Julia is appreciative of Sara's tolerance.

Unit A10: Travel
Exercise 1
1. adjacent
2. famous
3. far
4. excited
5. unsuitable

Exercise 2
1. with
2. for
3. from
4. about
5. for

Exercise 3
1. to
   The children stayed in a room adjacent to ours.
2. with
   We were the only tourists unfamiliar with Setswana.
3. for
   The city famous for skyscrapers is New York.
4. for
   You should buy shoes suitable for walking.
5. for
   Tom is the only student ready for today's tour.
6. about
   There are many students excited about the trip.

Exercise 4
1. for
   She's homesick for familiar faces and places.
2. for
   They are bound for the Everglades.
3. for
   New Orleans is famous for Mardi Gras.
4. about
   The children are excited about their trip to Yellowstone.
5. to
   The post office is adjacent to the public library.
6. for
   Formal clothing is suitable for the occasion.

Exercise 5
1. It is far from crowds.
2. It is not far from fun.
3. It is adjacent to the San Juan Marina.
4. Yes, there's something for everyone to get excited about.
5. It is famous for peace, quiet, and fun.
6. Everyone should be bound for the San Juans.

Unit A11: Trouble
Exercise 1
1. confused
2. suspicious
3. nervous
4. upset
5. afraid

Exercise 2
1. of
2. of
3. about
4. about
5. of

Exercise 3
1. of
   Suspicious of the strange-looking boy, they called the police.
2. about
   Confused about her location, she took out her compass and map.
3. about
   Nervous about her wedding, she decided to call her mother.
4. of
   Ashamed of his outburst, he planned to write a letter of apology.
5. of
   Afraid of walking at night, they decided to call a taxi.
6. about
   Anxious about her freshman year, she planned to visit the campus during the summer.

Exercise 4
1. about
   The diplomat is apprehensive about her meeting tomorrow.
2. of
   I am suspicious of the butler.
3. about
   My daughter is upset about her sick puppy.
4. about
   Mr. Hanson is troubled about his mother's failing health.
5. about
   She's anxious about the audit.
6. of
   The parents are fearful of their son's involvement in a gang.

Exercise 5
1. No, she is not upset about the mayor's decision.
2. He is afraid of abuses.
3. He is suspicious of the mayor's decision.
4. He might be confused about the procedures the council usually follows.
5. She thinks the council has nothing to be anxious about.
6. He is apprehensive about the ramifications of the mayor's decision.

Noun Phrases

In some exercises, more than one answer may be correct. Suggested answers are provided here.

Unit B1: Family Life
Exercise 1
1. dependence
2. quarrel
3. patience
4. influence
5. help

Exercise 2
1. for
2. of
3. with
4. of

Exercise 3
1. quarrel with
2. photograph of
3. help with
4. dependence on

Exercise 4
1. dependence on me
2. quarrels with each other
3. help with your project

Exercise 5
1. of depending
2. of complaining
3. of quarreling
4. of doing
5. of denying

Exercise 6
1. with
2. with
3. of
4. on
5. with

Exercise 7
1. Lila took pictures of Lenny and Eva.
2. Lila appreciated her grandfather's patience with her.
3. Eva asked Lila for help with everything.
4. Lila's parents' love for their children was remarkable.
5. The relationship between Lila's parents was loving.
6. Eva had a habit of asking for help with everything.

Unit B2: Entertainment
Exercise 1
1. concert
2. cancellation
3. postponement
4. books
5. show

Exercise 2
1. of
2. about
3. of
4. of

Exercise 3
1. postponement of
2. exhibit of
3. songs of
4. cancellation of
5. exhibit of

Exercise 4
1. of chamber music.
2. of cards.
3. about national parks.
4. about dinosaurs.

Exercise 5
1. about flying helicopters
2. about surviving a hurricane
3. about growing up in a small town
4. about being a single mother
5. about building ships
6. about working in a factory

Exercise 6
1. about
2. about
3. about
4. of
5. about

Exercise 7
1. On Saturday at 4:00, I could play a game of chess at Memorial Park.
2. Louie Lewis sings songs of love and despair.
3. The play about Henry IV is at City Theater.
4. The movie about ghosts starts at 8:00.

Unit B3: Language Learning
Exercise 1
1. pronunciation
2. practice
3. errors
4. fluency
5. translation

Exercise 2
1. in
2. of
3. of
4. with

Exercise 3
1. proficiency in
2. understanding of

3. pronunciation of
4. knowledge of
5. fluency in
6. translation of

Exercise 4
1. proficiency in English
2. knowledge of the language
3. error in the translation
4. understanding of the story
5. fluency in Greek
6. translation of the joke

Exercise 5
1. with
2. in
3. of
4. in
5. for

Exercise 6
1. Natalie's knowledge of the language and understanding of the culture are commendable.
2. Mr. Rupert will always remember Natalie's eloquent translation of Rilke's poetry.
3. Natalie needs more practice with spoken English.
4. Mr. Rupert thinks Natalie's fluency in English will improve.

Unit B4: Employment
Exercise 1
1. application
2. contract
3. layoff
4. connection
5. consideration

Exercise 2
1. for
2. in
3. of
4. against

Exercise 3
1. consideration of
2. notification of
3. application for
4. characteristic of
5. competence in
6. strike against

Exercise 4
1. contract for the job
2. employment of three new secretaries
3. connection with anybody
4. consideration of your proposal
5. notification of the pay raise
6. applications for the job

Exercise 5
1. with
2. for
3. in
4. of
5. against

Exercise 6
1. XYZ Industries is anticipating the employment of thirty workers.
2. The consideration of applications will last two months.
3. Enthusiasm and drive are the characteristics of a good applicant.

Unit B5: Harm and Safety
Exercise 1
1. danger
2. freedom
3. awareness
4. destruction
5. defense

Exercise 2
1. from
2. against
3. of
4. of

Exercise 3
1. destruction of
2. defense against
3. awareness of
4. neglect of
5. protection from
6. safety from

Exercise 4
1. safety from harm
2. protection from the authorities
3. neglect of their parental duties
4. awareness of the war
5. defense against attack
6. destruction of the forest

Exercise 5
1. What do we have freedom from?
2. What did they increase awareness of?
3. What is Vitamin C a defense against?

Exercise 6
1. We use sunscreen for protection from the sun's harmful rays.
2. We use fire alarms for safety from fires.
3. Bike locks provide defense against bike thieves.
4. Flotation devices can lessen the danger of drowning.

Unit B6: Friends and Enemies
Exercise 1
1. contact
2. disagreement
3. confidence
4. alliances
5. betrayal

Exercise 2
1. against
2. over
3. of
4. of

Exercise 3a
1. appreciation of
2. betrayal of
3. aggression toward
4. triumph over
5. alliance with
6. association with

Exercise 3b
1. confide in
2. have confidence in

Exercise 4a
1. association with the club
2. agreement with you
3. alliance against us
4. appreciation of our friendship
5. betrayal of your country
6. triumph over everyone

Exercise 4b
Usually when a verb is not followed by a preposition, *of* follows the noun. In this case, *with* is used.

Exercise 5
1. What did she have a disagreement with her teacher about?
2. Who did they have an alliance with?
3. Who had great confidence in him?
4. Who have you been in contact with?
5. Who led his team to victory over France?

Exercise 6
1. Everyone was in agreement with Lilly.
2. Lilly told everyone about Sandra's acceptance of a new job.
3. Lilly apologized for the possible betrayal of a secret.
4. She should be in contact with Stefan if she wants tickets.

Unit B7: Education

Exercise 1
1. paper
2. exam
3. study
4. instruction
5. analysis

Exercise 2
1. of
2. in
3. on
4. of

Exercise 3
1. analysis of
2. major in
3. study of
4. education of
5. instruction in
6. test on

Exercise 4a
1. education of the teenagers
2. test in social studies
3. major in geology
4. study of ancient paintings
5. analysis of the sentence
6. quiz on chapter 1

Exercise 4b
Of is used when the object form refers to someone; *in* is used when the object form refers to something.

Exercise 5
1. What does she have a major in?
2. What was his research on?
3. What did you write a paper on?
4. What are they taking courses in this semester?
5. Who did a study of Gothic architecture?

Exercise 6
1. Julia's study of motivation is due on Thursday.
2. Her paper on women poets is due on Tuesday.
3. Julia takes a quiz on algebraic equations on Wednesday.
4. She presents her research on motivation on Friday.

Unit B8: Business

Exercise 1
1. tax
2. price
3. order
4. production
5. bill

Exercise 2
1. for
2. of
3. for
4. on

Exercise 3a
1. production of
2. distribution of
3. charge of
4. credit of
5. cost of

Exercise 3b
of

Exercise 3c
On and *for* are used instead of *of*, even though the verbs are not followed by prepositions.

Exercise 4
1. credit of $70
2. charge of $100
3. distribution of overtime
4. order for new desks
5. price of the product
6. tax on everything

Exercise 5
1. What was the check for?
2. How much was the bill for?
3. What was the bill for?
4. What did they charge tax on?

Exercise 6
1. The cost of the building was $75,000. With tax, the cost of the building was $80,775.
2. The price of the carpet was $800. With tax, the price of the carpet was $861.
3. The tax on the carpet was $61.
4. The bill for the furniture was $2,154.
5. The price of the lights was $1,000. With tax, the price of the lights was $1,077.

Unit B9: Health

Exercise 1
1. growth
2. improvement
3. diagnosis
4. injection
5. prescription

Exercise 2
1. against
2. for
3. of
4. for

Exercise 3
1. treatment for
2. vaccination against
3. prescription for
4. diagnosis of
5. injection of
6. cure for

Exercise 4
1. cure for your illness
2. prescription for an ointment
3. growth in the number of kidney donors
4. vaccination against polio
5. injection of Novocain
6. treatment for your condition

Exercise 5
1. What is the best treatment for the flu?
2. Who never received a vaccination against the measles?
3. What department is she the head of?
4. What has there been a growth in this year?
5. When will Mary's prescription for eye drops be delivered?

Exercise 6
1. Yes, he received a prescription for Dermalotion.
2. Yes, the prognosis for recovery is good.
3. He will see improvement in his condition in three to four days.

Unit B10: Science and Technology
Exercise 1
1. argument
2. rationale
3. expert
4. deviation
5. difference

Exercise 2
1. in
2. for
3. for
4. on

Exercise 3
1. deviation from
2. competition for
3. connection between
4. difference between
5. superiority in
6. argument for

Exercise 4
1. for supporting the investigation
2. in designing software
3. against building a new factory
4. for creating user-friendly software
5. between eating fatty foods and suffering from heart disease
6. on manufacturing that product

Exercise 5
1. for
   Did he have a good argument for investing?
2. in
   Is she an expert in amphibian anatomy?
3. for
   Is there fierce competition for the $10,000 prize?
4. between
   Did they find a connection between the robbery and someone in her office?
5. on
   Does that company have a monopoly on baseball bats?

Exercise 6
1. Experts in space travel from Mid-Cosmos Corporation reported evidence for life on Mars.
2. Their argument included rationale for government subsidies.
3. The corporation has been accused of having a monopoly on space-travel vehicles.
4. The employees of Mid-Cosmos Corporation are experts in space travel.

Unit B11: Economy
Exercise 1
1. rise
2. damage
3. cause
4. fall
5. advantage

Exercise 2
1. for
2. in
3. in
4. in

Exercise 3
1. solution to
2. damage to
3. demand for
4. rise in
5. decrease in
6. cause of

Exercise 4
1. cause of the recession
2. damage to our relations with that country
3. demand for more funding for education
4. solution to our economic problems
5. fall in the value of their currency
6. increase in employment opportunities

Exercise 5
1. in
   Is the president worrying about a fall in stock prices?
2. for
   Is there high demand for employees with technical skills?
3. to
   Will the task force propose a solution to the crisis?
4. of
   Is the failing economy the cause of the tension between the government and the people?
5. in
   Did he recommend a cut in spending?

Exercise 6
1. Yes, there has been a rise in inflation.
2. Yes, a solution to the deficit has been reported.

3. Damage to the economy has been attributed to the International Trade Agreement.
4. No, there hasn't been any rise in the unemployment rate.
5. The president is promising a cut in taxes.

Prepositional Phrases

In some exercises, more than one answer may be correct. Suggested answers are provided here.

Unit C1: Time
Exercise 1
1. date
2. date
3. while
4. times
5. time
6. time
7. once
8. meantime
9. once
10. day, age

Exercise 2
1. At
2. for
3. out of
4. on
5. In
6. For
7. in
8. in

Exercise 3
1. The plane was on time.
2. For once, my dog actually came when I called her.
3. Toss the pasta with the oil and serve it at once.
4. We arrived in time to find front-row seats.
5. This machine is out of date.
6. His plane wasn't scheduled to leave for three hours, so in the meantime, he played video games.
7. At times my mom suffers from terrible headaches.
8. Let's think about this for a while before we make our decision.

Exercise 4
1. Erin isn't on time.
2. I could listen to the choir in the meantime. I could get a free hot dog and pop in the meantime.
3. Joe won't arrive in time to get a free hot dog.
4. I should go to the Atrium at once.
5. I could listen to the Jazz Band for a while.

Unit C2: Sequence
Exercise 1
1. start
2. line
3. addition
4. order
5. place
6. place, place
7. sum
8. end
9. point
10. conclusion

Exercise 2
1. At
2. In
3. For
4. in
5. out of
6. in
7. in
8. In

Exercise 3
1. In conclusion, I'd like to urge you all to attend tonight's debate.
2. The files are out of order.
3. In addition, he barred them from attending faculty meetings.
4. For a start, there's Disney World.
5. They will take no further action at this point.
6. The fans stood in line outside the ticket booth.
7. In the first place, financial predictions are hard to make. In the second place, we persuaded him to take a job he didn't want.
8. The students are listed in order according to their last names.

Exercise 4
1. At this point (in time), they park their cars on both sides of the street.
2. In addition, many of the Oak Street residents would have to go out of their way to get to the main thoroughfare.
3. They will have to wait in line at Dale Avenue to make a left turn.
4. In the first place, cars would go faster because they would be able to pass slower drivers. And fast cars might hit children crossing the street to visit their friends. In the second place, when cars go fast, they are noisy.

Unit C3: Buying and Selling
Exercise 1
1. check
2. sale
3. stock
4. cash
5. rent
6. sale
7. free
8. credit card
9. line
10. nothing

Exercise 2
1. by
2. on
3. by
4. for
5. for
6. in
7. for
8. on

Exercise 3
1. We don't have any printer ribbons in stock right now.
2. They bought their dining-room table on sale.
3. He has $15 in cash.
4. There will be T-shirts for sale after the concert.
5. They were moving, so they gave us their old couch for free.
6. We couldn't pay by credit card, so we had to pay in cash.
7. Because of the hot summer, fans were out of stock by the second week in July.
8. You can pay by check.

Exercise 4
1. There are canoes, kayaks, and hiking gear for rent at Trek Sporting Goods.
2. It will be replaced for free.
3. Repairs are done for nothing.
4. Weather radios are on sale at Trek Sporting Goods.
5. If you want to order a tent on line, you should go to the website at www.treksport.com.
6. Payments are made by check or credit card.

Unit C4: Similarities and Differences
Exercise 1
1. contrast
2. common
3. ways
4. comparison
5. contrary
6. contrary
7. hand, hand
8. hand
9. way
10. odds

Exercise 2
1. In
2. by
3. at
4. in
5. On
6. On
7. in
8. to

Exercise 3
1. They are in no way related.
2. We are at odds.
3. They had nothing in common.
4. They were told I spoke fluent Spanish. On the contrary, I hardly speak any Spanish.
5. He published a statement to the contrary.
6. We might be able to win the game tonight. On the one hand, we have two home-run hitters. On the other hand, one of them is ill.
7. Children begin to speak when they reach a certain point in their development. In the same way, they begin to read when they are developmentally ready.
8. There are many old buildings in Eastern cities. In contrast, the skylines of Western cities include very few old buildings.

Exercise 4
1. Yes, the two plans have something in common. Both plans include a library exhibit.
2. In Plan A, dinner is for students and faculty only. In contrast, in Plan B, everyone in town is invited.
3. No, on the contrary, Xiaoying wants to have lunch language demonstrations.
4. It will be larger by comparison.
5. They are similar in every way. In both plans, arts and crafts from around the world will be exhibited.

Unit C5: Health
Exercise 1
1. weather
2. diet
3. health
4. spirits
5. pain
6. shape
7. medication
8. breath
9. therapy
10. mend

Exercise 2
1. in
2. on
3. under
4. in
5. out of
6. in
7. on
8. in

Exercise 3
1. Many people in the region are in poor health.
2. He is in high spirits because he found out he can leave the hospital tomorrow.
3. The doctor said I was out of shape.

4. The patient was in pain, so he was given ibuprofen.
5. We're happy to know that you're on the mend.
6. I don't know why I am out of breath.
7. Are you on a diet? You look thinner.
8. What are you on medication for?

Exercise 4
1. The staff is in high spirits because the clinic has programs and equipment to help the employees of Hi-Tech Industries.
2. They are for employees who want to get in shape or stay in shape.
3. Employees who want to get in shape or stay in shape might want to use the exercise machines.
4. An employee who wants to go on a diet might want to consult a nutritionist.
5. An employee in low spirits can talk to a counselor.
6. No, they can be in good or poor health.

Unit C6: Entertainment
Exercise 1
1. suspense
2. radio
3. tour
4. town
5. fun
6. concert
7. town
8. vacation
9. lunch
10. television

Exercise 2
1. For
2. on
3. for
4. in
5. on

6. in
7. in
8. on

Exercise 3
1. in concert
2. for dinner
3. out of town
4. on the radio
5. in suspense
6. on vacation
7. For fun
8. on television

Exercise 4
1. They are going to Pike Place Market for breakfast.
2. The Mariners baseball team is in town this week.
3. They are going to hear Mel Corley in concert.
4. For fun, they are going to go up the Space Needle and visit the amusement park.
5. They could go on a tour of the Seattle Art Museum.
6. They are going to the Fish Bar for dinner on Sunday evening.

Unit C7: Perspectives
Exercise 1
1. record
2. view
3. point
4. perspective
5. course
6. fact
7. perspective
8. record
9. fact
10. opinion

Exercise 2
1. Off
2. into
3. In
4. In
5. beside
6. In

7. For
8. as

Exercise 3
1. As a matter of fact
2. off the record
3. In their view
4. Of course
5. From my perspective
6. in fact
7. beside the point
8. into perspective

Exercise 4
1. Many of her friends do not have computers at home. In fact, they often have to stay on campus late to finish computer work.
2. He thinks the designers of the policy need to put their proposal into perspective.
3. He says that, of course, students need to be computer literate, but the proponents of the policy have to remember what students can afford.
4. From Mike's perspective, the proposal is a good one.
5. Because of his limited work with computers, he's not hirable. As a matter of fact, he was told recently during an interview that he should take some computer classes before he continued his job search.
6. In Sandra's view, the college should try to make it possible for students to have easy access to computers.

Unit C8: Process
Exercise 1
1. point
2. road

3. verge
4. process
5. search

Exercise 2
1. to
2. in
3. In
4. by
5. in

Exercise 3a
1. at, of
2. In, of
3. in, of
4. on, of
5. on, to
6. in, of
7. in, of
8. in, of
9. by, of

Exercise 3b
Most of the multiword prepositions in this unit follow this pattern: Preposition + Noun Phrase + Preposition + Noun Phrase.

Exercise 4
1. at the point of
2. in the middle of
3. on the verge of
4. on the road to
5. In the course of
6. in the process of
7. by means of
8. in search of
9. in pursuit of
10. prior to

Exercise 5
1. In the course of her studies, she has gained experience in both computer systems and financial applications.
2. Prior to working at the university computer center, she worked as an intern for a large bank.
3. It is a firm in pursuit of excellence.
4. No, she is at the point of finishing her program.

Unit C9: Location
Exercise 1
1. top
2. door
3. front
4. middle
5. back

Exercise 2
1. in
2. of
3. of
4. of
5. on

Exercise 3
1. across from the pharmacy
2. in front of the school
3. in between the buildings
4. in back of the groom's family
5. next door to her best friend
6. on top of the telephone pole
7. ahead of the tourists
8. outside of the window
9. inside of the cave
10. in the middle of the pool

Exercise 4
1. of
It is on top of the public library.
2. to
He lives next door to Travis.
3. of
I was sitting in back of Terry.
4. of
They were ahead of the Craigs.
5. of
I was waiting outside (of) the Frost Building
6. of
They sat in front of their old friends at the ceremony.
7. of
He hid inside (of) the wooden one.

8. from
She lived across from the apartment superintendent.

Exercise 5
1. She has her desk in front of the window.
2. She keeps a picture of her family on top of the desk to remind her of home.
3. It is in the middle of the living room.
4. It is on a table in back of the sofa.
5. It is in front of the sofa.
6. It is so big that you can walk inside (of) it.

Unit C10: Exceptions and Substitutions
Exercise 1
1. spite
2. exception
3. lieu
4. spite
5. place

Exercise 2
1. of
2. from
3. of
4. for
5. for

Exercise 3a
Two-Word
    apart from
    except for
    instead of
    irrespective of
    regardless of
    save for
Three- or Four-Word
    in lieu of
    in place of
    in spite of
    with the exception of
Nouns are found in three- or four-word phrasal prepositions but not in two-word phrasal prepositions.

Exercise 3b
1. instead of
2. Irrespective of
3. With the exception of
4. except for
5. regardless of

Exercise 4a
Possible answers include:
1. Instead of speaking softly, the professor should tell an exciting story.
2. Except for having to give speeches, I like the class.
3. In spite of yawning a lot, the professor engages the students in discussions.
4. In place of assigning speeches, the professor should ask us to write a final paper.
5. In lieu of giving only a final exam, the professor should give weekly quizzes.
6. Apart from having too much homework, my classmates enjoy the course.

Exercise 4b
gerund (verb + *ing*)

Exercise 5
1. Save for the dinner, everything has been planned.
2. Except for Mr. Hermann, everyone has been sent an invitation.
3. Ms. Lamont will give the tour in place of Ms. Green.
4. In lieu of an outdoor picnic, we've planned lunch at the Garden Cafe.
5. Instead of meeting in the morning, our visitors would like to meet after lunch.
6. Apart from a free hour in the morning, the visitors will have very little free time.

Unit C11: Decisions
Exercise 1
1. sake
2. view
3. respect
4. favor
5. result

Exercise 2
1. In
2. of
3. As
4. On

Exercise 3
1. For the sake of
2. As a consequence of
3. with a view toward
4. Owing to
5. In view of
6. as a result of
7. Because of
8. on account of
9. Out of respect for
10. in favor of

Exercise 4
1. As a consequence of turning in your paper late
2. with a view toward enlarging it later
3. On account of his complaining
4. in favor of establishing a day care at the factory
5. because of misbehaving on the playground
6. as a result of receiving a scholarship
7. For the sake of building a strong community
8. as a consequence of not fulfilling her responsibilities
9. As a result of investing their money wisely
10. in favor of increasing the speed limit

Exercise 5
1. There were many accidents owing to bad roads.
2. He is in favor of a new amendment.
3. The police were called in as a result of the students' riot.
4. He's opening up a food shop now with a view toward opening up a restaurant later.
5. They are being cautious on account of the storm warnings.
6. It was postponed because of rain.

Unit C12: Reference
Exercise 1
1. regard
2. wake
3. reference
4. case
5. respect

Exercise 2
1. for
2. of
3. with
4. in
5. on

Exercise 3
1. As for
2. In case of
3. in reference to
4. in relation to
5. In light of
6. on behalf of
7. In regard to
8. In the wake of
9. In keeping with
10. With respect to

Exercise 4a
Possible answers include:
1. In keeping with what we have done in the past, I'd like to say a few words.

2. With respect to what she has argued, I'd like to raise an issue.
3. With respect to what they have proposed, I'd like to ask a question.
4. In regard to what she has argued, I agree.
5. In light of what we have done in the past, I'd like to say a few words.

Exercise 4b
noun clause

Exercise 5
1. With respect to businesses in financial trouble, Roosevelt established the National Recovery Administration.
2. With regard to unemployed youth, Roosevelt established the Civilian Conservation Corps.
3. In regard to underdeveloped resources, Roosevelt established the Tennessee Valley Authority.
4. In the wake of the bombing of Pearl Harbor, Roosevelt declared war.
5. In light of severe unemployment, Roosevelt established the Public Works Administration and the Works Progress Administration.

Verb Phrases

These are suggested answers. In some cases, other answers are possible.

Unit D1: Friends
Exercise 1
1. live
2. know
3. talk

4. share
5. happen

Exercise 2
1. with
2. for
3. to
4. about
5. about

Exercise 3a
1. with Alan
2. about Wanda's accident
3. to your car
4. for another flight
5. with each other

Exercise 3b
1. He knows about their reputation.
2. My friend lives with her parents.
3. She cares about her pets.
4. Something wonderful happened to Julia today.
5. I heard about his good luck.

Exercise 4
1. chatted with
2. laughed about
3. waited for
4. talked with
5. gossiped about

Exercise 5
1. with
2. about
3. about
4. with
5. for

Exercise 6
1. Lise is living with Mina and Jessie.
2. Mina and Jessie's friend is sharing an office with Lise.
3. They want to hear about Eduardo and his family.
4. They were laughing about old times.
5. They are waiting for Eduardo's letter.

Unit D2: School
Exercise 1
1. read
2. think
3. lecture
4. listen
5. report

Exercise 2
1. on
2. about
3. of
4. about
5. on

Exercise 3a
1. We read about it in the newspaper.
2. They listened to us.
3. She reported on it.

Exercise 3b
1. She wrote about him.
2. I didn't listen to them.
3. The article focuses on her.

Exercise 3c
No. In declarative sentences and yes/no questions, the verb and the preposition in a prepositional verb must not be separated.

Exercise 4
1. reported on
2. focused on
3. talked about
4. concentrated on
5. lecture on

Exercise 5
1. of
2. to
3. about
4. on
5. on

Exercise 6
1. The course focuses on music.
2. They listen to many types of music that are

currently popular in the United States.

3. On Mondays, the teacher lectures on specific topics.
4. On Wednesdays, the class talks about an assigned reading.
5. On Fridays, students report on their own research.
6. At the end of the course, students must write about some type of music they have studied.

Unit D3: Working Together

Exercise 1
1. argue
2. talk
3. work
4. depend
5. side

Exercise 2
1. with
2. on
3. about
4. with
5. to

Exercise 3
1. to . . . about
2. with . . . about
3. with . . . against
4. on . . . for
5. with . . . on

Exercise 4
1. relied on
2. complained to
3. disagreed about
4. talk about
5. argued about

Exercise 5
1. I depend on my friend for help.
2. She complained to the manager about her salary.
3. She complained to the manager about her salary.
4. I worked with him on the marketing project.

Exercise 6
1. They talked about their work to the director.
2. We argued with management about employee benefits.
3. The workers spoke about their jobs to a union representative.
4. I worked with Merlin on the design.

Exercise 7
1. They argue about their duties.
2. No, she can't speak to her supervisor about her concerns.
3. She doesn't like Vern because he always complains about the rest of the workers to the supervisor.
4. They work on projects together.
5. They disagree about office assignments.

Unit D4: Shopping

Exercise 1
1. shop
2. look
3. glance
4. ask
5. search

Exercise 2
1. at the price
2. at the funny T-shirt
3. for help
4. at them

Exercise 3a
at: glance, laugh, point, stare, look
for: ask, beg, look, search, shop

Exercise 3b
At implies direction.
For implies need or desire.

Exercise 4
1. I'm laughing at these funny ties.
2. I'm looking for long-sleeved T-shirts.
3. I asked for my receipt.
4. I'm pointing at the silver one.

Exercise 5
1. your daughter has been begging for
2. you're looking for
3. you were looking at
4. he asked for
5. she was shopping for

Exercise 6
1. She should shop for sandals for her son at Lundy's.
2. He should look for a cheap pair of sneakers at Lundy's.
3. She should ask for help choosing wedding shoes at Jamaica's High Fashion.
4. He should shop for work shoes at Lundy's.
5. She should look at the latest shoe styles at Jamaica's High Fashion.
6. Rolf looked for golf shoes at Mark's Sporting Goods.

Unit D5: Dating

Exercise 1
1. go
2. ask
3. feel
4. pick
5. break

Exercise 2
1. up
2. for
3. up
4. like
5. out

Exercise 3
1. He'll call up the girl this afternoon.
2. They are going out tonight.
3. Let's make up.
4. He asked his friend over to celebrate the end of his project.
5. She's been going with him for several years.

Exercise 4
1. ask . . . over
2. ask . . . out
3. fall for / go with
4. pick . . . up
5. call . . . up
6. make up

Exercise 5a
1. I feel like skiing today.
2. Let's pick up your friend at 6:00. *or* Let's pick your friend up at 6:00.
3. He's been going with her for years.
4. Did you ask both couples over?

Exercise 5b
1. I feel like having a cup of coffee.
2. Laura went with him for seven years.
3. He can pick up Karin at 7:00. *or* He can pick Karin up at 7:00.
4. You fall for someone different every month.

Exercise 6
1. Paul fell for Marta.
2. Marta was going with Lars.
3. Paul is asking Marta over for dinner.
4. He's going to call Min up.
5. He's going to pick them up at 6:00.

Unit D6: Travel
Exercise 1
1. get
2. check
3. wake
4. Pack
5. get

Exercise 2
1. off
2. up
3. out
4. out
5. up

Exercise 3
1. Did your rental car break down?
2. I must get back early in the day.
3. We got by without a guide.
4. We woke up in a new place.
5. Should we gas up the car?

Exercise 4
1. wake up
2. check in
3. tire . . . out
4. get by
5. gas up

Exercise 5
1. in/out
2. out
3. back
4. by
5. off

Exercise 6
1. check out
2. take off
3. break down
4. check in

Exercise 7
1. Check-in was at 9:30.
2. He forgot to set his alarm because he got back from the party so late the night before.
3. He woke up at 7:30.

4. He forgot his Walkman because he packed up his things so fast.
5. Something on the plane broke down.
6. The plane took off at 2:00.

Unit D7: Family
Exercise 1
1. hear
2. take
3. look
4. get
5. take

Exercise 2
1. into
2. down
3. away
4. up
5. from

Exercise 3
1. get along
2. pass away
3. hand . . . down
4. look after
5. take up

Exercise 4
1. The spoiled child grew into a monster.
2. He handed down a great legacy. *or* He handed it down.
3. The parents heard from all of their children regularly.
4. I'll look after the goldfish while you're away.
5. They both take after Uncle Louie.

Exercise 5a
1. up
2. away
3. up
4. up
5. into

Exercise 5b
1. The relative <u>you take after the most</u> is your great-grandfather.
2. The children <u>I look after every day</u> are my sister's.
3. The town <u>where he grew up</u> was very small.
4. The daughter <u>I heard from yesterday</u> lives in Mexico City.
5. I never met the uncle <u>I take after</u>.

Exercise 6
1. The kids don't take after either Susan or Jack.
2. No, she hasn't heard from Susan recently.
3. He might take up meteorology.
4. Greg passed away.
5. She is surprised by what interesting kids Alec and Andrew have turned into.
6. She would like to hear from Linda.

Unit D8: Weather
Exercise 1
1. cool
2. let
3. put
4. set
5. warm

Exercise 2
1. off
2. up
3. off
4. off
5. off

Exercise 3a
1. Why don't you put on a wide-brimmed hat?
2. Why don't you call off the game?
3. Why don't you put on your raincoat?
4. Why don't you call off the meeting?

5. Why don't you take off your sunglasses?

Exercise 3b
1. Why don't you put it on?
2. Why don't you call it off?
3. Why don't you put it on?
4. Why don't you call it off?
5. Why don't you take them off?

Exercise 3c
They are separated: verb + pronoun + particle.

Exercise 4
1. When is it going to dry off?
2. When is it going to let up?
3. When is it going to warm up?
4. When is it going to cool off?
5. When is it going to clear up?

Exercise 5
1. They should put on raincoats today.
2. It will let up by tomorrow morning.
3. A high-pressure system will set in.
4. It will clear up and dry off. It will probably cool off a bit, too.
5. We should put on sweaters.
6. It will warm up.

Unit D9: Entertaining
Exercise 1
1. see
2. Pick
3. look
4. get
5. go

Exercise 2
1. away
2. up
3. over
4. up
5. out

Exercise 3
1. Yes, stir it up.
2. Yes, clear them away.
3. Yes, let's let Lucy pick them out.
4. Yes, let's have them over.
5. No, serve them up in about ten minutes.

Exercise 4
1. off
2. to
3. up
4. over
5. up

Exercise 5
1. He/she picked out decorations two weeks before the party. *or* He/she picked decorations out two weeks before the party.
2. He/she dished up the salad. *or* He/she dished the salad up.
3. He/she cleared away the dishes. *or* He/she cleared the dishes away.
4. He/she ate up everything. *or* He/she ate everything up.
5. He/she cooked up the pasta in ten minutes. *or* He/she cooked the pasta up in ten minutes.

Exercise 6
1. The cake batter was stirred up.
2. The guests were seen off.
3. The ripest tomatoes were picked out.
4. The mess was cleared away.
5. All the rolls were eaten up.

Exercise 7
1. He looked up the recipes.
2. He mixed up the ingredients for the spring rolls.
3. He should stir it up.
4. He should cook up the potatoes.
5. He picked out some small candles.
6. Binh should serve up the appetizers, and Alberto should dish up the dessert.

Unit D10: Business
Exercise 1
1. fall
2. pay
3. shut
4. buy
5. sell

Exercise 2
1. in
2. off
3. out
4. up
5. through

Exercise 3
1. off
2. up
3. down
4. up
5. up
6. in

Exercise 4
1. bail out
2. lay off
3. pay off
4. shut down
5. sell off

Exercise 5
1. The cost of the equipment wasn't figured in.
2. The restaurant wasn't opened up until 5:00.
3. They were bailed out.
4. Our old office building was finally sold off.
5. The plant in Kansas was shut down.

Exercise 6
1. The factory in Pasco shut down.
2. The gas station opened up every day at 6:00.

Exercise 7
1. He will shut down out-of-state stores.
2. Existing stores will open up copy centers.
3. He will buy up manufacturers' low-priced items.
4. He thinks he should pay off his loans.
5. A hundred employees at in-state stores will be laid off.
6. He will sell off the inventory from out-of-state stores.

Unit D11: Discussion
Exercise 1
1. hear
2. bring
3. Quiet
4. talk
5. cut

Exercise 2
1. out
2. up
3. up
4. around
5. over

Exercise 3
1. The gossip shut up immediately when a friend came into the room.
2. Could you speak up?
3. The owner shouted down the union representative.
4. The children finally quieted down.
5. Let's talk over the matter.

Exercise 4
1. to hear you out
2. to speak up
3. to cut in
4. to speak out

Exercise 5
1. Ernie shouted them down.
2. We'll hear them out.
3. He talks around it.
4. We talked it over.
5. Did anyone bring it up?

Exercise 6
1. Who was the person who brought up personal topics?
2. Who was the person who never spoke up?
3. Who was the person who talked around the topic of library funding?
4. Who was the person who never shut up for very long?
5. Who was the person who didn't hear me out?

Exercise 7
1. Alice brought up the topic of local pollution.
2. Simon has spoken out in the past on that topic.
3. Anton cut in.
4. Simon was not heard out.
5. Rita was asked to speak up.
6. She wanted to talk over the issue of pollution control.

Unit D12: Training
Exercise 1
1. fill
2. look
3. get
4. keep
5. come

Exercise 2
1. up
2. along
3. up
4. out
5. in

Exercise 3
1. up with
2. forward to
3. up on
4. along with
5. in for

Exercise 4a
1. A retired manager filled in for our trainer.
2. I haven't kept up with the recent changes.
3. She brushed up on nutrition for her nursing exam.
4. They came up with an astonishing design.
5. The students looked forward to finishing their program.

Exercise 4b
It always occurs after the verb and before the preposition.

Exercise 5
1. Let's come up with
2. Let's read up on
3. Let's keep up with
4. Let's fill in for
5. Let's study up on

Exercise 6
1. Who does he get along with?
2. What did you get out of?
3. What are you looking forward to?
4. What is she reading up on?
5. What did they come up with?

Exercise 7
1. You should keep up with current thought in our field.
2. You should come up with original ideas.
3. You shouldn't always ask other people to fill in for you.
4. You should study up on necessary research.
5. You shouldn't always get out of doing your share of the work.
6. You should read up on important procedures.

Index

Note: Numbers in parentheses refer to unit numbers.

a

absent from something (A3)
acceptance of someone (B6)
accomplished at something (A8)
accustomed to someone or something (A7)
across from someone or something (C9)
add something up (D10)
adjacent to something (A10)
advantage of something (B11)
afraid of someone or something (A11)
aggression toward someone (B6)
agree with someone / about something (D3)
agreement with someone (B6)
ahead of someone or something (C9)
akin to something (A4)
alliance against someone (B6)
alliance with someone (B6)
amazed by someone or something (A1)
amused by something (A5)
analysis of something (B7)
angry at someone (A5)
anxious about something (A11)
apart from something (C10)
application for something (B4)
appreciation of someone or something (B6)
appreciative of something (A9)
apprehensive about something (A11)
argue with someone / about something (D3)

argument against something (B10)
argument for something (B10)
as a consequence of something (C11)
as a matter of fact (C7)
as a result of something (C11)
as for something (C12)
ashamed of someone or something (A11)
ask for something (D4)
ask someone out (D5)
ask someone over (D5)
association with someone (B6)
at odds (C4)
at once (C1)
at the point of doing something (C8)
at this point (C2)
at times (C1)
attached to someone or something (A6)
attracted to someone or something (A6)
aware of something (A7)
awareness of something (B5)

b

bail someone or something out (D10)
beg for something (D4)
because of something (C11)
beguiled by someone or something (A1)
beside the point (C7)
betrayal of someone or something (B6)
bewitched by someone or something (A1)
bill for something or some amount (business) (B8)
blessed with something (A8)
book about someone or something (B2)

bored with something (A7)
bound for somewhere (A10)
break down (Travel) (D6)
break up (D5)
bring someone or something up (Family) (D7)
bring something up (Discussion) (D11)
brush up on something (D12)
buy something up (D10)
by check (C3)
by comparison (C4)
by contrast (C4)
by credit card (C3)
by means of something (C8)

c

call someone up (D5)
call something off (D8)
cancellation of something (B2)
capable of something (A7)
captivated by someone or something (A1)
care about someone or something (D1)
care of someone (B1)
cause of something (B11)
chance of something (B5)
characteristic of someone or something (B4)
charge of some amount (B8)
charmed by someone or something (A1)
chat with someone (D1)
check for something or some amount (B8)
check in (D6)
check out (D6)
clear something away (D9)
clear up (D8)
close to someone (A6)
cloud up (D8)
come up to something (D12)
come up with something (D12)

comfortable with someone or something (A2)

comparable to something (A4)

competence in something (B4)

competent in something (A4)

competition for something (B10)

complain to someone/about someone or something (D3)

concentrate on something (D2)

concert of something (B2)

confidence in someone or something (B6)

confident of something (A8)

confused about something (A11)

connected to something (A4)

connection between some things (B10)

connection with someone (B4)

consideration of something (B4)

contact with someone (B6)

content with something (A2)

contented with someone or something (A2)

contingent upon something (A4)

contract for something (B4)

cook something up (D9)

cool off (D8)

cost of something (B8)

course in something (B7)

credit of some amount (B8)

cure for something (B9)

cut in (D11)

cut in something (B11)

d

damage to someone or something (B11)

danger of something (B5)

decrease in something (B11)

dedicated to someone or something (A3)

defense against someone or something (B5)

delighted with something (A2)

demand for something (B11)

depend on someone or something (for something) (D3)

dependence on someone (B1)

dependent on someone or something (A4)

destruction of something (B11)

deviation from something (B10)

devoted to someone or something (A6)

diagnosis of something (B9)

difference between some things (B10)

different from something (A9)

disadvantage of something (B11)

disagree with someone/about something (D3)

disagreement with someone (B6)

disappointed in someone or something (A2)

discontented with someone or something (A2)

disgusted with something (A5)

dish something up (D9)

displeased with something or someone (A2)

dissatisfied with something or someone (A2)

distribution of something (B8)

drink something up (D9)

dry off (D8)

e

eat something up (D9)

education of someone (B7)

employed at someplace (A3)

employment of someone (B4)

enamored of someone or something (A6)

enchanted by someone or something (A1)

endowed with something (A8)

engaged in something (A7)

engaged to someone (A6)

enthralled by someone or something (A1)

entranced by someone or something (A1)

envious of someone or something (A5)

error in something (B3)

evidence against something (B10)

evidence for something (B10)

exam(ination) on something/ in a subject (B7)

except for someone or something (C10)

excited about something (A10)

exhibit of something (B2)

expert at something (A8)

expert in something (B10)

f

fall in something (B11)

fall for someone (D5)

fall through (D10)

familiar with something (A10)

famous for something (A10)

far from somewhere (A10)

fascinated by someone or something (A1)

fearful of something (A11)

fed up with something (A5)

feel like something (D5)

figure something in (D10)

fill in for someone or something (D12)

film about someone or something (B2)

fluency in something (B3)

focus on something (D2)

fond of someone or something (A6)

for a start (C2)

for a while (C1)

for breakfast (C6)

for dinner (C6)

for free (C3)

for fun (C6)

for lunch (C6)

for nothing (C3)

for once (C1)

for rent (C3)

for sale (C3)

for the record (C7)

for the sake of something (C11)

freedom from something
(B5)
from someone's perspective
(C7)
fuel something up (D6)
furious with someone or
something (A5)

g
game of something (B2)
gas something up (D6)
get along (D7)
get along with someone
(D12)
get back (D6)
get by (D6)
get out of something (D12)
get to something (D9)
gifted with something (A8)
glance at something (D4)
good at something (A8)
good of someone (A9)
go out (D5)
go over (D9)
go with someone (D5)
gossip about someone or
something (D1)
grateful to someone / for
something (A9)
grow into someone or
something (D7)
grow up (D7)
growth in something (B9)

h
habit of doing something
(B1)
hand something down (D7)
happen to someone or something (D1)
happy about something (A2)
have someone over (D9)
head of something (B9)
hear about someone or something (D1)
hear from someone (D7)
hear someone out (D11)
help with something (B1)
hike in something (B11)
homesick for something
(A10)

i
impatience with someone
(B1)

impressed with someone
or something (A3)
improvement in something
(B9)
in a bind (C13)
in addition (C2)
in back of someone or something (C9)
in between some people or
somethings (C9)
in case of something (C12)
in cash (C3)
in common (C4)
in concert (C6)
in conclusion (C2)
in contrast (C4)
in every way (C4)
in fact (C7)
in favor of something (C11)
in front of someone or something (C9)
in good health (C5)
in high spirits (C5)
in keeping with something
(C12)
in lieu of something (C10)
in light of something (C12)
in line (C2)
in low spirits (C5)
in many ways (C4)
in no way (C4)
in order (C2)
in pain (C5)
in perspective (C7)
in place of someone or something (C10)
in poor health (C5)
in pursuit of something (C8)
in reference to something
(C12)
in regard to something (C12)
in relation to something
(C12)
in search of something (C8)
in shape (C5)
in some ways (C4)
in someone's opinion (C7)
in someone's view (C7)
in spite of something (C10)
in stock (C3)
in sum (C2)
in suspense (C6)
in the course of something
(C8)
in the end (C2)

in the first place (two phrases)
(C2)
in the meantime (C1)
in the middle of something
(two phrases) (C8) (C9)
in the process of doing something (C8)
in the same way (C4)
in the second place (C2)
in the wake of something
(C12)
in therapy (C5)
in this day and age (C1)
in time (C1)
in town (C6)
in view of something (C11)
incapable of something (A7)
incompetence in something
(B4)
incompetent in something
(A3)
increase in something (B11)
indebted to someone (for
something) (A9)
independent of someone or
something (A4)
infatuated with someone (A6)
inferiority in something (B10)
influence on someone (B1)
injection of something (B9)
inside (of) something (C9)
instead of someone or something (C10)
instruction in something (B7)
interest in something (B7)
into perspective (C7)
intolerant of something (A7)
irrelevant to something (A4)
irrespective of something
(C10)

j
jealous of someone or something (A5)

k
keep up with something (D12)
kind of someone (A9)
know about someone or
something (D1)
knowledge of something (B3)

l
laugh about something
(D1)

laugh at something (D4)
lay someone off (D10)
layoff of someone (B4)
learn about someone or something (D2)
lecture on something (D2)
let up (D8)
listen to someone or something (D2)
live with someone (D1)
look after someone or something (D7)
look at something (D4)
look for something (D4)
look forward to something (D12)
look something up (D9)
love for someone (B1)

m
mad at someone (A5)
major in something (B7)
make up (D5)
married to someone (A6)
mix something up (D9)
monopoly on something (B10)
movie about someone or something (B2)

n
necessary for something (A3)
neglect of something (B5)
nervous about something (A11)
next door to someone or something (C9)
nice of someone (A9)
notification of something (B4)

o
of course (C7)
off the record (C7)
okay with someone or something (A2)
on a diet (C5)
on a tour (of somewhere) (C6)
on account of something (C11)
on behalf of someone (C12)
on line (C3)
on medication (C5)
on sale (C3)

on television/TV (C6)
on the contrary (C4)
on the mend (C5)
on the one hand (C4)
on the other hand (C4)
on the radio (C6)
on the road to something (C8)
on the town (C6)
on the verge of something (C8)
on time (C1)
on top of something (C9)
on vacation (C6)
open something up (D10)
open to something (A7)
order for something (B8)
out of breath (C5)
out of date (C1)
out of order (C2)
out of perspective (C7)
out of respect for someone or something (C11)
out of shape (C5)
out of stock (C3)
out of town (C6)
outside (of) something (C9)
owing to something (C11)

p
pack something up (D6)
paper on something (B7)
pass away (D7)
patience with someone (B1)
pay something off (D10)
photograph of someone or something (B1)
pick someone up (D5)
pick something out (D9)
picture of someone or something (B1)
play about someone or something (B2)
pleased with something or someone (A2)
point at something (D4)
postponement of something (B2)
practice with something (B3)
prepared for something (A3)
prescription for something (B9)
price of something (B8)
prior to something (C8)
production of something (B8)

proficiency in something (B3)
prognosis for something (B9)
promise of something (B7)
pronunciation of something (B3)
protection from something (B5)
proud of something (A7)
put something on (D8)

q
qualified for something (A3)
quarrel with someone (B1)
quiet down (D11)
quiz on something/in a subject (B7)

r
rationale for something (B10)
read about something (D2)
read up on someone or something (D12)
ready for something (A10)
reason for something (B11)
reduction in something (B11)
regardless of something (C10)
related to someone or something (A4)
relationship between persons (B1)
relevant to something (A4)
rely on someone or something (for something) (D3)
report on something (D2)
required of someone (A3)
research on something (B7)
responsible for something (A7)
rise in something (B11)
rule for something (B3)

s
safety from someone or something (B5)
satisfied with something or someone (A2)
save for someone or something (C10)
search for something (D4)
security against someone or something (B5)
see someone off (D9)
sell something off (D10)
sensitive to something (A9)
serve something up (F9)

set in (D8)

share something with someone (D1)

shop for something (D4)

shout someone down (D11)

show about someone or something (B2)

shut something down (D10)

shut up (D11)

sick of something (A5)

side with someone/against someone or something (D3)

similar to something (A4)

solution to something (B11)

song of something (B2)

sorry for something (A9)

speak out (D11)

speak to someone/about something (D3)

speak up (D11)

stare at someone or something (D5)

stir something up (D9)

strike against someone or something (B4)

study of something (B7)

study up on someone or something (D12)

suitable for something (A10)

suited to something (A3)

superiority in something (B10)

sure of someone or something (A8)

suspicious of someone or something (A11)

t

take after someone (D7)

take off (D6)

take something off (D8)

take something up (D7)

taken with someone or something (A6)

talented at something (A8)

talk about something (D2)

talk around something (D11)

talk something over (D11)

talk to someone/about something (D3)

talk with someone (D1)

tax on something (B8)

test on something/in a subject (B7)

thankful for something (A9)

think of something (D2)

thoughtful of someone (A9)

tied to something (A4)

tire someone out (D6)

tired of something (A5)

to date (C1)

to the contrary (C4)

tolerant of something (A7)

translation from something into something else (B3)

translation of something (B3)

treatment for something (B9)

triumph over someone or something (B6)

troubled about something (A11)

u

unaccustomed to someone or something (A7)

unafraid of someone or something (A11)

unashamed of someone or something (A11)

unaware of something (A7)

uncomfortable with someone or something (A2)

under the weather (C5)

understanding of something (B3)

uneasy about something (A2)

unfamiliar with something (A10)

unhappy about something (A2)

unimpressed with someone or something (A3)

unite with someone or something/against someone or something (D3)

unnecessary for something (A3)

unprepared for something (A3)

unqualified for something (A3)

unrivaled in something (A8)

unsuitable for something (A10)

unsuited to something (A3)

upset about something (A11)

used to someone or something (A7)

v

vaccination against something (B9)

victory over someone or something (B6)

video about someone or something (B2)

w

wait for someone or something (D1)

wake up (D6)

warm up (D8)

with a view toward something (C11)

with reference to something (C12)

with regard to something (C12)

with respect to something (C12)

with the exception of someone or something (C10)

work with someone/on something (D3)

write about something (D2)